IMPACT OF GADGET USAGE ON PRESCHOOL CHILDREN

By

Dr. Sowmya ASL

Founder and Trainer

Spurthi Pre-Primary Educational Academy (SPPEA)

Hyderabad (Telangana)

(India)

&

Dr. Manjuvani E.

M.Ed., M.Phil., Ph.D.

Professor

Department of Human Development and Family Studies

Sri Padmavati Mahila Visvavidyalayam (SPMVV)

Tirupati (Andhra Pradesh)

(India)

DPH

DISCOVERY PUBLISHING HOUSE PVT. LTD.

INDIA

Published by:
Namit Wasan

DISCOVERY PUBLISHING HOUSE PVT. LTD.
4383/4B, Ansari Road, Darya Ganj
New Delhi-110 002 (India)
Phone : +91-11-23279245; 23253475; 43596065
E-mail : discoverybooksindia@gmail.com
discoverypublishinghouse@gmail.com
namitwasan9@gmail.com
web : www.discoverypublishinggroup.com

***First Edition:* 2021**

ISBN: 978-93-88854-67-2

Impact of Gadget Usage on Preschool Children

Printed at:
Infinity Imaging Systems
Delhi

Preface

"The connections in the brain fade away unless used. We know that early stimulation of children leads to higher cognitive scores"

– *Brian Sutton-Smith*

As I kept earning my degrees and gaining experience in the field of Early Childhood Education, I began to recognize the importance of stimulation in the early years. I have been observing a radical change on aspects related to childhood as we are moving from non-digital to the digital era. Earlier, children had lots of social opportunities to live in the joint families, play with friends and explore. Now the amount of time children are spending with people has come down and time spent with gadgets has increased. This concern developed an interest in me to do the research in this area and write this book. Linguistic and social skills are the most important developmental domains during the early years. Hence the study was carried out to understand the influence of children's usage of electronic gadgets on these areas.

This book describes the intensive literature review, process of research carried out, findings and implications of the study. In chapter four, I have stated the statistical figures on how preschool age group children are spending time with different electronic gadgets. I have also written about perceptions of mothers and preschool teachers on children's usage of electronic gadgets. This chapter further deals with identifying the association between preschool children's gadget usage and their language development, social skills and problem behaviour. Chapter five will enable you to understand the implications for parents, schools, Government and NGO sectors.

I am grateful to my research supervisor Prof. E. Manjuvani, Department of Home Science, SPMVV, Tirupati and all others who have helped me directly and/or indirectly in preparing this book. I am thankful to Discovery Publishing House Pvt. Ltd. for the opportunity of getting associated with them to publish this book.

Dr. Sowmya ASL

Preface

Acknowledgements

I place my deep sense of gratitude and regard to my Research Supervisor Prof. E.Manjuvani, Department of Home Science, SPMVV, Tirupati for her valuable guidance and suggestions in publishing this book. I extend my gratitude to the entire staff members in the department of Home Science for their support. I acknowledge gratitude towards Sri Padmavati Mahila Visvavidyalayam, Tirupati for the facilities provided to carry out my research and publishing this book. I express my sincere gratitude to Mr. Amit Kishore Prasad for his support and mothers, teachers and children who participated in the research work. Without their cooperation, it would be impossible to carry out my research. I would like to express my heartfelt sense of love and honours to my family and friends for their motivation, moral support and constant encouragement. Finally, a very special thanks to Discovery Publishing House Pvt. Ltd., for the opportunity of getting associated with them to publish this book.

Contents

Abstract

Electronic gadgets have become an integral part in our daily lives. As adults become increasingly more dependent and absorbed technology, today's children have become avid users as well. Children below six years of age are becoming experts at using technology and will become the first generation of active digital natives from a very early age.

In a survey conducted by the Erikson Institute (2016), technology use by young children under age 6 was found to be almost universal. In this study of thousand parents, 85% reported that they allow their young children to use technology. Television, tablets, smartphones and computers were the most popular. According to UNICEF, 2017 report, "Internet use among children is increasing. Children are spending more time online and using digital devices at ever-younger ages. At the same time, children's online access is becoming more personal, more private and less supervised".

Young children usage of technology has a positive impact on their learning however it sometimes can impede their development. The present research is aimed to study the *"Impact of Gadget Usage on Preschool Children"*.

The study has adopted exploratory research design in Hyderabad city, Telangana State. The sample consists of 200 preschool children, 200 mothers and 60 preschool teachers. Five research tools – Availability and usage of electronic gadgets questionnaire, Perceptions of mothers towards children usage of electronic gadgets questionnaire, Perceptions of teachers towards children usage of electronic gadgets questionnaire, Language development tests (LDT) and Preschool and kindergarten behaviour scales (PKBS2) were used to obtain the data.

The results reveal that almost all families are having television set (99%) and smart phones (99.5%) at home. Nearly one fourth (23.5%) of preschool children are having their own tablet/IPad and 10% owned game consoles. Usage of electronic gadgets is high in 20% of preschool children during working day whereas it is almost doubled (39%) during holiday. When the age increases, children usage of electronic gadgets on holiday has been increased significantly. Boys are spending more time with gadgets on a holiday as compared to girls. Similarly, fathers are spending more time with electronic gadgets when compared with mothers on both working day and holiday.

Mothers of below 30 years group, undergraduates and working have more positive perceptions towards gadgets usage of preschool children. Whereas, mothers belong to above 30 years age group, post graduates and non-working are more concerned about children health issues and gadget addiction.

Same as mothers, below 30 year age group teachers have shown more positive perceptions on children usage of electronic gadgets and above 30 year age teachers raised concern about children sleeping disturbances. Undergraduate teachers have more positive perceptions that gadget usage is helpful for children's attention, concentration and entertainment while post graduate teachers perceived gadget usage causes sleeping disturbances among children.

The findings are evident that when the age increases, language development of 3 to 6 year old children is increased significantly. Preschool girls scored higher on all language tests as compared to boys. The results found that children with high gadget usage scored higher on language development tests than children with low gadget usage.

There is significant association between preschool children age, gender and their social skills. Social skills of the children increased with their increase in age. Girls scored higher on social cooperation, social interaction and social independence than boys. Children who are spending less time with electronic gadgets during working day and holiday scored higher on social skills as compared with high gadget usage children.

There is an association between age and problem behaviour of 3 to 6 year old children. In contrast, there is no association between gender and problem behaviour of preschool children. Children with high electronic gadgets usage scored higher on problem behaviour subscales than low gadget usage children on both working day and holiday.

It can be concluded from the findings that electronic gadgets have both positive and negative influence on preschool children. Excessive screen time impede children social skills and causes problem behaviour. There is a need for continued education of parents about harmful effects of children's excessive usage of electronic gadgets. Parental monitoring and time regulation are most important aspects to be considered. Parents need to engage their children with a variety of indoor and outdoor games and spend quality time. This is helpful for parent-child bonding and holistic development of preschool children.

1

Introduction

A child's early years are the foundation for later stages and provide a strong base for lifelong development in the physical, cognitive, linguistic and socio-emotional domains. Neurological research shows that preschool stage plays a key role in child's brain development. Development psychologists attach great importance to this stage because this is a period of mental growth. What parents do and expose their children to, will have a vast impact on the development of the child.

Parents are the first mentors and role models for children. During early childhood period, children imitate and learn skills from parents. So parents have an immense contribution and responsibility in shaping child's personality. Positive parenting promotes healthy growth of children. Particularly mothers can greatly influence child's development. Mothers have an extremely important role in child rearing. The amount of time they spend with children during early years make an impact on child's progress. Besides parents, teachers play an impeccable role in child's life. They not only influence children but also parents.

Today's children are fascinated with electronic gadgets such as television, smart phone, tablet, IPad, laptop, computer, game console etc. Mostly children use gadgets for entertainment purpose like watching cartoons, videos, browsing and playing games. It is also a fact that parents allow children to spend time with gadgets to keep them quite in one place for a period of time.

We can see children not getting tired by spending time with gadgets even though they use for longer hours. This obsession is definitely a concern for parents and educators. When children use gadgets, they do not pay attention to their screen distance, brightness, body posture which may affect their health. Technology is definitely a boon for children but parental monitoring and control is essential.

CHILDREN USAGE OF ELECTRONIC GADGETS

A growing body of research indicates that the time spent by children with electronic gadgets has been increased significantly over the world. "Children and adolescents below eighteen years are estimated one in three internet users around the world. Smartphones are fuelling a 'bedroom culture' and online access has become more personal, more private and less supervised. Digital gender difference found worldwide. Twelve percent more number of male used the internet in 2017 as compared to female. In India, less than one third of internet users are female" (UNICEF report, 2017).

'Every year more and more children are spending time with modern digital media technology. It can be seen as a clear trend that some form of mobile technology usage begins at an early age. Usage of tablets has increased twice in 2014, as compared to 2012-2013. In Sweden, there are 56% of children at the age of 0-1 years, 79% of children at the age of 2-4 years and 84% at the age of 5-8 years have access to a tablet computer' (Swedish Media Council report, 2015).

In an Indian study, it was found that 90% of children were eating food while watching television and 33% were eating fast foods at least once a week. Majority (59%) children skipped outdoor activities for watching television (Priyadarshini *et.al*, 2013).

Undoubtedly electronic media has impact on young children. Children and adolescents are influenced by media – they learn by observing, imitating and making behaviours on their own (American Academy of Paediatrics, 2009). 'Although many children turn into relatively competent users of technologies already at a young age, parents or other caregivers are still facilitators, teachers and gatekeepers of young children's media use' (Chiong and Shuler, 2010). So it is important to understand parents and teachers attitudes and views towards children usage of technology.

PARENTS' AND TEACHERS' VIEWS ON CHILDREN USAGE OF ELECTRONIC GADGETS

Parental perceptions on usage of electronic gadgets by children have an influence on their screen time. Consequently, positive opinions and concerns of parents have become thrust area for researchers. Levels of concern among preschool parents have increased – comparatively more parents than in 2016 said that they are concerned about their child's media use across TV, online, mobile phones and gaming (Ofcom report, 2017).

Children are spending significantly more time with touch screens and have more electronic screens in their bedrooms when their parents agreed that the media provide a moment of rest. Parental attitudes about the effects of media on children are important predictors of the parents' mediation strategies. Parents who agreed with the positive influence of media especially more often applied supervision, co-use and active mediation, whereas parents who were concerned about negative effects more often supervised, restricted and used technical restrictions on the young child's media behaviour (Nikken and Schols, 2015).

Keeping aside concerns, parents and teachers have positive attitudes towards their children usage of electronic gadgets. 'Parents and teachers have positive perceptions on children usage of educational apps. The total percentage of parents believed that mobile educational math apps can increase the maths skill level of their children and most of the teachers also believed that mobile apps can increase the maths skill level of their learners' (Venter *et.al*, 2016).

Similarly, parents and teachers have positive perceptions towards the use of computers, the internet and social networking sites. However researchers suggested that supervision by parents, information controlling and school policies play a crucial part for regulating children usage time (Penjuree and Penjira, 2012).

Young children are active users of electronic gadgets but they cannot discriminate between the reality and fantasy. "The effects of the electronic media found to be far reaching and potentially harmful in influencing the health related behaviours of children many of whom are not yet mature enough to distinguish fantasy from reality, particularly when it is presented as real life. Electronic media has a disturbing potential which affects negatively on many aspects like children's weight status, aggressive feelings, beliefs and social isolation etc" (Ray and Kana, 2010). Hence it is important to understand the influence of electronic gadgets on child's development.

INFLUENCE OF ELECTRONIC GADGETS ON CHILD'S LANGUAGE DEVELOPMENT AND SOCIAL SKILLS

During preschool age, child's linguistic and social developments are crucial for their communication. Hence studying the impact of children's screen time on these two domains is essential.

The presence of background television was 'in addition to affecting the quantity of parent-child interactions, it also affects the quality of interactions. Verbal responses were described as passive in nature with parents verbally acknowledging without looking or not responding to their children. Because the quality of verbal responses is reduced in the presence of background television, it is plausible that parents and caregivers are not providing the same types of language models that they may otherwise. A reduction in mature models could potentially have an effect on language development' (Kirkorian *et.al,* 2009).

In the same way, each hour of average daily television viewing before age three years was associated with deleterious effects of linguistic development of children's reading recognition and comprehension of later ages (Zimmerman and Christakis, 2005).

'Children who watch more television may sleep less or have poorer quality sleep which may subsequently reduce their ability to be calm, disrupting their capacity to be compliant and behave appropriately in social situations' (Hinkley *et.al.* 2018).

Screen time not only impacts children's social development but also their problem behaviour and capacity to pay attention via several mechanisms as it leads to sleep disturbances and adversely impacts brain development. The number of hours spent viewing television at a young age has been linked with future attention difficulties (Parent *et.al,* 2016).

There is a strong link between violence in video games and real life violence. Video games lead to social isolation and lack of communication and communication with children (Kutner and Olson, 2008).

Developmentally appropriate programs would enhance children's learning. Excessive screen time impedes children's language development and social skills.

NEED AND IMPORTANCE FOR THE STUDY

Despite negative impact of screen time on children's development, parents are not regulating their children's usage time. Most children and adolescents live in homes where there are no parental rules regarding screen time.

Parents were more likely to have rules regarding programs viewed but even then nearly half of the children and adolescents stated that there were such rules in their home. In majority of the homes, television was left on during meal time and in nearly half of the houses television was left on most of the time in a day. Only one third of children and adolescents stated there were household rules regarding time spent viewing television. (Kaiser Family Foundation Study, 2010). Therefore parental control of children screen time is very important.

Preschool age is the fundamental stage in the human lifespan with rapid growth and development. It is essential to educate parents on experts' recommended screen time for preschoolers and how to divert children from gadgets and engage them with a variety of activities.

There is limited literature available on preschool age group children, their parents and teachers in the context of electronic gadget usage. Thus it is important to study the usage of electronic gadgets among preschool children and its influence on their developmental domains.

The present study will be useful for parents and educators to understand the role of electronic gadgets usage and their impact on language and social development of preschool children. This study will be helpful for early childhood policy makers for making changes in the curriculum framework and planning educational programmes for parents.

STATEMENT OF THE PROBLEM

"Usage of Electronic Gadgets among Preschool Children and their Language Development, Social Skills and Problem Behavior"

THEORETICAL BACKGROUND

A theoretical perspective is a logical system of general concepts that underlies the organization and understanding of observations. It helps to explain how people change and grow over time, as well as how to account for continuity. It offers a language of constructs and hypotheses that guide systematic inquiry and compare observations in order to build a body of knowledge.

Theories of Language Acquisition

"Language is a cognition that truly makes us human. Language acquisition is the process by which humans acquire the capacity to perceive and comprehend language, as well as to produce and use words and sentences to communicate" (Friederici, 2011).

Skinner Theory

One of the earliest scientific explanations of language acquisition was provided by Skinner (1957). "As one of the pioneers of behaviourism, he accounted for language development by means of environmental influence. Skinner argued that children learn language based on behaviourist reinforcement principles by associating words with meanings. Correct utterances are positively reinforced when the child realizes the communicative value of words and phrases" (Lemetyinen, 2012).

Noam Chomsky Theory

However, Skinner's account was soon heavily criticized by Noam Chomsky, the world's most famous linguist to date. "The most well-known theory about language acquisition is the *Nativist theory,* which suggests that we are born with something in our genes that allows us to learn language. It proposes that there is a theoretical *language acquisition device (LAD)* somewhere in our brains that is responsible for learning a language the same way the hypothalamus is responsible for maintaining your body temperature.

Consequently, he proposed the theory of *Universal Grammar*: an idea of innate, biological grammatical categories, such as a noun category and a verb category that facilitate the entire language development in children and overall language processing in adults." (Lemetyinen, 2012).

Jean Piaget Theory

"Piaget theorized that language is made up of symbols and structures, but exhibits itself as a child's mental abilities mature. In addition, language is only one of many human mental or cognitive activities. Piaget's view of how children's minds work and develop has been enormously influential, particularly in educational theory. His particular insight was the role of maturation in children's increasing capacity to understand their world, they cannot undertake certain tasks until they are psychologically mature enough to do so" (Wanjohi, 2010).

Theories of Social Development

According to Bilance (1997) "social development is the promotion of a sustainable society that is worthy of human dignity by empowering marginalized groups, women and men to undertake their own development, to improve their social and economic position and to acquire their rightful place in society".

Vygotsky Theory

"Vygotsky's theory is one of the foundations of constructivism. It asserts three major themes regarding social interaction, the more knowledgeable other, and the *Zone of proximal development*. Social interaction plays a fundamental role in the process of cognitive development. In contrast to Jean Piaget's understanding of child development, Vygotsky felt social learning precedes development. He stated that every function in the child's cultural development appears twice - first, on the social level and later on the individual level. The ZPD is the distance between a student's ability to perform a task under adult guidance and/or with peer collaboration and the student's ability solving the problem independently" (David, 2014).

Kegan's Theory

Kegan described a theory of how people become progressively more socially mature across their lifespan. His *social maturity* theory suggested that "as babies grow into adults, they develop progressively more objective and accurate appreciations of the social world they inhabit. They do this by progressing through five or more states or periods of development which he labeled as *Incorporative, Impulsive, Imperial, Interpersonal* and *Institutional*. In their beginnings, babies are all subjective and have really no appreciation of anything objective at all, and therefore no real self-awareness. They can recognize parent's faces and the like, but this sort of recognition should not be confused with babies being able to appreciate that parents are separate creatures with their own needs. This key recognition doesn't occur for years" (Kegan, 1982).

Bandura's Social Learning Theory

"The social learning theory of Bandura emphasizes the importance of observing and modelling the behaviours, attitudes and emotional reactions of others. Learning would be exceedingly laborious, not to mention hazardous, if people had to rely solely on the effects of their own actions to inform them what to do. Fortunately, most human behaviour is learned observationally through modelling: from observing others one forms an idea of how new behaviours are performed, and on later occasions this coded information serves as a guide for action" (Bandura, 1977).

Problem Behaviour Theory

According to Jessor (1977) "Problem behavior is the behavior that is socially defined as a problem, as a source of concern, or as undesirable by the social and/or legal norms of conventional society and its institutions of authority; it is behavior that usually elicits some form of social control response, whether minimal, such as a statement of disapproval, or extreme, such as incarceration".

Jessor's Problem Behavior Theory

"The conceptual structure of problem-behavior theory is both complex and comprehensive. The theoretical framework included three major systems of explanatory variables – the perceived environment system, the personality system and the behavior system. Each system is composed of variables that serve either as instigations for engaging in problem behavior or controls against involvement in problem behavior. Within each explanatory system, it is the balance of instigations and controls that determines psychosocial proneness for involvement in problem behavior and it is the balance of instigations and controls across the three systems that determines the adolescent's overall level of problem behavior proneness or psychosocial unconventionality" (Donovan, 2005).

The above theories emphasized that children's language development, social skills and problem behaviour are influenced by environmental factors and their psychological maturity. Thus the theories are helpful in understanding the definitions and concepts of language development, social skills and problem behavior.

OBJECTIVES

1. To assess the usage of electronic gadgets among preschool children.

2. To study the perceptions of mothers towards children usage of electronic gadgets.
3. To study the perceptions of the teachers towards children usage of electronic gadgets.
4. To compare the language development of low and high electronic gadget usage preschool children.
5. To compare the social skills of low and high electronic gadget usage preschool children.
6. To compare the problem behaviour of low and high electronic gadget usage preschool children.

NULL HYPOTHESES

HO 1.1. Age has no effect on the usage of electronic gadgets among preschool children.

HO 1.2. Preschool boys and girls do not differ on the usage of electronic gadgets.

HO 2.1. Mothers' age has no effect on their perceptions towards children usage of electronic gadgets.

HO 2.2. Mothers' education has no effect on their perceptions towards children usage of electronic gadgets.

HO 2.3. Mothers' working status has no effect on their perceptions towards children usage of electronic gadgets.

HO 3.1. Teachers' age has no effect on their perceptions towards children usage of electronic gadgets.

HO 3.2. Teachers' education has no effect on their perceptions towards children usage of electronic gadgets.

HO 4. Low and high electronic gadget usage preschool children do not differ significantly on their language development.

HO 5. Low and high electronic gadget usage preschool children do not differ significantly on their social skills.

HO 6. Low and high electronic gadget usage preschool children do not differ significantly on their problem behaviour.

2

Review of Literature

A comprehensive view of literature plays a vital role for any investigation. It not only gives an idea on the work done in the subject but also provides basis for interpretation and discussion of findings. An intense effort has been made to review the relevant research findings that have direct or indirect influence on the present study.

CHILDREN USAGE OF ELECTRONIC GADGETS

Technology has become an integral part in our daily lives. These include Smart phones, Television, Computer, Laptop, Tablet, IPad, Video games and different types of other electronic gadgets. As adults become increasingly more dependent and absorbed technology, today's children have become avid users as well. Children below six years of age are becoming experts at using technology and will become the first generation of active digital natives from a very early age.

According to International Telecommunications Union 2015 report, almost 3.2 billion people of the world's current population are online. In a survey conducted by the Erikson Institute (2016), technology use by young children under age 6 was found to be almost universal. In this study of 1,000 parents, 85% reported that they allow their young children to use technology. Television, tablets, smartphones, and computers were the most popular.

Ofcom survey reported that among the families with children below 8 years, 72% of children had used a mobile device to play games, watch movies or use apps. It also found that 29% of 3-4 year olds had used a computer or laptop at home, 12% used a tablet to go online, and 58% had online to access games (Ofcom Report, 2013).

Another research claimed that 13% of 3-4 year olds spend over 4 hours a day in front of screens at home (Fletcher *et.al*, 2014). Barr and Lerner (2014) found that 38% of children under the age of 2 had used a mobile device, in comparison to 10% in 2012. Thus the largest increase in usage of mobile phones among two to four year old children was 80% in 2014, where as it was 39% in 2012.

A study conducted by Vandewater *et.al.* (2007) demonstrated that screen media have become ubiquitous in the homes of very young children. They found that most children lived with at least two television sets in their home and nearly one fourth of children lived with four or more televisions in their home. In addition, 4 out of 5 young children were in homes with either cable or satellite access. Approximately half of households had a video game console, and between one ûfth (0 to 2 year old children) and one third (5 to 6 year old children) had access to a handheld video game. Seventy eight percent of households reported having a computer and 69% of households had Internet access.

Another survey reported that different ranges of technologies are available to children, with the television and DVD player being most common in the home. Unlike desktop and laptop computers, which were restricted to adult use in half of homes, smartphones and tablets were quite prevalent and generally available for children's use. This study reported that children used gadgets in different places at home like 38% in the home office area, 36% in the living room. Forty five percent of young children engaged independently with technology, able to accomplish activities and learn on their own. This study contributes to a growing body of literature about how young children connect to technology and the growing digital world around them (Given etal, 2014).

The above studies indicate that young children are exploring different electronic gadgets like television, tablets, smart phones and computers etc. The usage of technology among children has been increasing from year to year. Research has shown that, there are variations in screen time usage across the countries. The data of different countries is presented below.

The Anti-virus Guard digital diaries research revealed that several children below the age of nine had their Facebook account. They mentioned that *Italian* children had the highest percentage of children with Facebook account by 22% of the children, followed by *French* children having 15% of their children ("Young Children Report", 2011).

Brouwer *et.al* (2011) surveyed 575 parents in the *Netherlands*. They discovered that not only were touch screen technologies very popular with children aged 3-6, but parents reported that this age group were quick to master the touch and swipe access techniques. Although only 7% of families owned touch screens at the time of the survey, 11% have mentioned that they are going to buy one in the coming 12 months indicating 'a market which would be likely to double in size each year over the next two to three years with a specific focus on families with very young children'.

A year later, in *Norway*, researchers reported that 32% of below three years were already using touchscreens with 23% of 0-6 year olds having regular access to a touchscreen in their home (Guomundsdottir and Hardersen, 2012). These figures were slightly higher than in *Germany* where 17% of families with 3-7 year old children had touchscreen tablets compared with 18% of families where the children were 6-11 years old (Behrens and Rathgeb, 2012).

Disney *et.al.* (2013) presented results of an observational study of preschool children's use of iPads in childcare centers in *Australia*. They found that young children can engage actively with the iPad, enjoy playing with gadgets, and they can easily use the touch screen compared to traditional mouse and keyboard.

A study carried out in the *United States* found that 59% of the children had access to a tablet device, 52% to a games console and half had access to a smart phone. Forty eight percent had access to a Laptop computer and 42% had access to a desktop computer with access increasing with age (Almeida *et.al*, 2015). Another study from *Singapore* found that in the first two years of school all children had access to mobile phones (Goh *et.al*, 2015).

A cross-national analysis conducted by Chaudron (2015) on seven European countries (*Belgium, Germany, UK, Russia, Italy, Finland* and *Czech Republic*) revealed that children are growing up in media-rich homes. Tablets were found to be their favourite devices because size of its screen, portability and its ease of use. Smartphones are innovative in their use and allow children to watch videos, play games, send messages, take pictures and make video calls etc. The study also revealed that in most cases, children use their parents' device equipped with free apps in different context and different activities but recurrently for filling gaps in the day, to keep the children engaged during free time or when parents need to retrieve time for themselves.

The Pew Research Centre (2016) reported that as of 2015, ninety two percentage of *Americans* own a cell phone, with 68% owning a smart phone, and 45% have a tablet of some type. These numbers have drastically increased in recent years. According to the Pew Research Centre, in 2004 only 65% of Americans owned a cell phone, in 2011 only 35% of adults owned a smart phone, and in 2010, only 3% of American adults owned a tablet.

Bansal and Mahajan (2017) conducted a survey on 450 *Indian* children and the findings show that ninety six percent children were using either parents' or relative's mobiles. The study showed that only eight percent of children have never used mobiles. Majority (43%) of the children were using mobiles for 1-3 hours followed by 29% children those who used mobile for more than 4 hours. Nearly forty three percentage of the children were using mobile for playing games, followed by 35% watching YouTube videos and 25% children were surfing internet. In fifty percent of cases, mobile was given to children to tackle with the tantrums and in 37% cases mobiles were given to keep them engaged.

Thus the various studies conducted in different countries showed the statistics on availability and usage of electronic gadgets among the families with young children. Children are operating the devices with ease and they are using them for playing games, watching videos, surfing internet etc. Parents are allowing children to use the gadgets to tackle with their tantrums and keep them occupied.

Among all electronic gadgets, television continues to be the most commonly used form of media, cell phones and tablets are quickly becoming a close second in overall usage (Barr and Lerner, 2014). Zimmerman and Christakis (2005) found a detrimental effect of overall TV viewing on reading recognition, reading comprehension and memory for digit span for television viewing before age 3 but a beneficial effect of TV viewing on reading recognition at ages 3 to 5 years. Linebarger and Walker (2005) argued that content is a stronger predictor of developmental outcomes than total time spent watching television.

Kaiser Family Foundation survey (2006) reported that 43% of children under one year old watch Television everyday and 72% of two and three year old children are daily TV viewers. Anderson and Pempek (2005) reported that when compared with the data from the 1980s and 1990s, the data from the Kaiser Family Foundation studies showed an extreme increase in the number of very young children attending to TV on an average day.

According to Nielsen's National Television Household Universe Estimates (2016), there were 116.4 homes in the United States with televisions for the 2015-2016 television season. They found that 95.2% of homes in the United States have television accessed through broadcast, cable, or internet connection, as compared to 96.1% in the 2014-2015 TV season. Another study demonstrated that children between the ages of birth to 2 years of age watch, on an average of 55 to 75 minutes of television per day and children between the ages of 2 and 4 years of age watch approximately 90 minutes per day (Blankson *et.al* 2015).

Duch *et.al* (2013) conducted a cross-sectional and longitudinal study on 119 Hispanic infants and toddlers. The research revealed that the children in this sample watched television for an average of 3.29 hours per day with 2.09 hours being child directed and 1.29 hours being adult-directed programs. As the children's age in this study increased, the amount of child-directed television viewing also increased. This study also looked at the types of technology being used in the homes and found that television was the most popular with cell phones being the second most popular form. The study also found that 35% of toddlers and 28% of infants used cell phones for a minimum of 30 minutes each day.

The above studies indicate that the majority of families with young children are equipped with one or more than one television sets at home. Access to broadcast, cable or internet connection has been increasing over the years. The findings also reveal the tremendous increase of television viewing by children per day.

Young children usage of technology has a positive impact on their learning however it sometimes can impede their development. The review with regard to positive and negative impact on children usage of electronic gadgets is presented below.

Children Usage of Electronic Gadgets and Positive Impact

Electronic gadgets are fun for children when they use them. Most of the gadgets are easy to use and have advanced options for children to play and learn. Technology has been proven to be very helpful in educating children. Many studies revealed that the technology had positive effect on children's performance across developmental domains.

In one study, screen media was found to be beneficial if two key factors – content and context were taken into consideration. They testified that learning from screen media takes place if the content is interactive and provides contingent responses to a child's actions. Another key factor is to ensure screen time is a positively shared experience where parents or caregivers need to help children to apply digital learning in their real life experiences (Barr and Lerner, 2014).

'Apart from the noticeable entertainment like playing games and watching videos, many young children are using gadgets for mingling online and their interaction with the internet is helpful to develop the trending digital literacies among the young children. It can also be supporting their future academic performance, such as data mining and social interaction wellbeing' (Cavanaugh *et.al*, 2004).

Touch screens promote independence and allow very young children to play in a self-directed and independent manner (Brouwer *et.al*, 2011).Young children can and do engage actively with technology on their own and gain a great deal of information from independent engagement (Setliff, 2009).

Young children learn from games and creative activities, they absorb information while engaging with fun tools. Downes found in her research of children between ages five and twelve, "children conceived of and used the computer as both a toy and a tool, and that when they were thinking of and using the computer as a tool, it was a 'playable' tool. Working with a playable tool provided opportunities for the blending of play, practice and performance" (Downes, 2002).

Results of an Indian study revealed that reading skills, watching television had a positive correlation irrespective of controlling for educational content or other forms of media exposure. Mathematics correlated positively, when children television watching durations was one and half to two in a day (Singh and Gaurav, 2012).

NAEYC (2009) emphasized the significance of providing preschool children with a variety of developmentally appropriate practices that encourage their self-esteem, independence, identity formation, and individual strengths. Developmentally appropriate practice means that teachers shift their focus from traditional teaching strategies and move toward providing experiences that align with children's needs, abilities, and love for learning.

Christakis *et.al.* (2013) suggested that "well designed, age-appropriate educational programs and screen activities can be powerfully pro-social and help children to learn anti-violence attitudes, empathy, tolerance and respect".

Heim *et.al* (2007) suggested that "when parents are actively involved in their child's daily activities, the child is more likely to embrace media for creative, educational purposes rather than as a medium for games or TV".

The above studies suggested that technology is beneficial to children if content and context are regulated. Age appropriate programmes will enhance children's learning, academic performance and independence. Contradicting the above findings, studies which showed the negative impact of usage of electronic gadgets on children is given below.

Children Usage of Electronic Gadgets and Negative Impact

Although technology provides many positive benefits for children learning, it also can have several negative effects on their health and quality of life. It depends on various factors such as parents' awareness, content monitoring and time regulation.

In 1982, NIMH published a 10-year follow-up of the 1972 Surgeon General's study. The two-volume report, collectively titled Television and Behaviour: Ten Years of Scientific Progress and Implications for the Eighties provided a reminder of the breadth and depth of knowledge that has accumulated on the issue of TV violence. In this regard, the NIMH staff and consultants concluded that after 10 more years of research, the consensus among most of the research community is that violence on television leads to aggressive behaviour by children and teenagers who watch the programs. The above conclusions are based on field studies and laboratory experiments. They mentioned that not all children become aggressive, but the correlations between violence and aggression are positive. In magnitude, television violence is as strongly correlated with aggressive behaviour as any other behavioural variable that has been measured (NIMH, 1982).

Chonchaiya and Pruksananonda (2008) conducted a study with a sample of 56 children with language delays and 110 children with normal language development, ages 15- to 48 months old. They asserted that children who started watching television before 12 months of age and watched more than 2 hour/day were six times more likely to develop a language delay. Although studies on the relationship between screen time and language development are few and mostly limited to observational or quasi-experimental methods, findings have remained consistent that increased screen time is associated with an increased risk for language developmental delays.

According to young and Abreu (2011), too much time on the internet can destructively influence numerous aspect of young children's lives possibly leading to non prioritization of important task, psychological problems like anxiety, lower self-esteem and physical health concerns due to lack of physical activities.

Waldman *et.al* (2006) reported that Autism is a complex disorder, thought to have a genetic basis which may be activated by other things. A study at Cornell University suggests that early childhood screen viewing may be such a trigger factor for autism.

Another research found that childhood television viewing was associated with attention problems in adolescence, independent of early attention problems and other confounders. These results support the hypothesis that childhood television viewing may contribute to the attention disorders and suggest that the effects may be long-lasting. These findings could not be explained by attention difficulties that occur in the early childhood stage, socio-economic factors or intelligence. The authors stated that even after all of these factors were taken into account, watching more television was associated with teenage attention problems (Landhuis *et.al.*, 2007).

The National Health and Nutrition Examination Survey included 2964 children ages 4 to 11 years and demonstrated a positive correlation between increased media use and increased adiposity (Anderson *et.al.* 2008). Rideout (2004) reported that a study of more than 13,000 children found evidence to suggest that for each additional one hour of TV viewing, there is a 2% increase in childhood obesity. This study adjusted for prior weight, socio-economic status, maternal weight, and race.

A research study in the medical journal paediatrics has examined the impact of only a small number of minutes of TV cartoon viewing on the intellectual functions carried out by the brain's frontal lobes in 4 year old children. These 'prefrontal' skills are referred to as a child's executive function which underlies goal-directed behaviour, including attention, working memory, inhibitory control, problem solving, self-regulation, and delay of gratification thus leading to positive social and cognitive functioning and their strong association with the child's success at school. The results were that 'Just 9 minutes of viewing a fast-paced television cartoon had immediate negative effects on 4-year-olds' executive function (Lillard and Peterson, 2011).

According to Barr (2010), "there is solid evidence that infants and toddlers have difficulty transferring new learning from a 2D representation to a 3D object (e.g., from screen to real life) and are unlikely to learn from TV at this age".

Lin *et.al* (2015) found that prolonged TV viewing was associated with lower cognitive abilities, especially related to short-term memory, early reading, math skills and language development. In another study, TV viewing has been found to be negatively associated with school readiness skills, especially as family income decreases (Ribner etal, 2017).

A study conducted by Thompson and Christakis (2005) on 2068 children found that television viewing among infants and toddlers was associated with irregular sleep patterns. The number of hours of television watched per day was independently associated with both irregular naptime schedule and irregular bedtime schedules.

In a study on five to six year olds, Paavonen *et.al.* (2006) found that both active TV viewing and background 'passive' TV exposure was related to shorter sleep duration, sleeping disorders, and overall sleep disturbances. It was also found that passive exposure to television of more than two hours per day was strongly related to sleep disturbances.

Ray and Kana (2010) observed that the media has a disturbing potential to negatively affect many aspects of children's healthy development, including weight status, sexual initiation, aggressive feelings and beliefs, consumerism and social isolation. Media also has potential for positive effects on child's health. They have suggested that parents and experts need to find ways to optimize the role of media in the society, taking advantage of their positive attributes and minimizing their negative ones. Instead of accepting the media as it is, regulating it helps to shape the behaviour of children and adolescents.

Technology and media should not replace activities such as creative play, real-life exploration, physical activity, outdoor experiences, conversation, and social interactions that are important for children's development. Technology and media should be used to support learning, not an isolated activity, and to expand young children's access to new content (Guernsey, 2012).

From the above studies it is evident that childhood obesity, violent behaviour, aggression and irregular sleep patterns positively co-relate with technology usage. The screen time of children depends upon parents' perceptions and attitudes towards their usage. The findings presented below show the perceptions of parents on children usage of electronic gadgets.

PERCEPTIONS OF PARENTS TOWARDS CHILDREN USAGE OF ELECTRONIC GADGETS

Parental involvement plays a key role on child's development during early childhood period. Parents are role models for children at this age group. Since parents are active users of technology, children are also getting attracted towards the gadgets. Numerous studies have looked at the parental perceptions towards children usage of electronic gadgets.

In one study consisting of 51 parents in Melbourne, Australia, "parents' responses revealed the importance they place on computer use and also their positive attitudes towards using technology". This study found that about half of parents consider computer use appropriate one time per week for children, while the other half of parents in this study believed once per week was not frequent enough. They expressed that exposure to electronic technology is vital to child's development and future success. (Hatzigianni and Margetts, 2014).

According to Erikson survey report (2016), majority of the parents mentioned that they use technology along with their child on a daily basis for up to two hours. Eighty six percent of them reported that they were satisfied with how their young children use technology, relating technology to benefits associated with child development and literacy. More than half of them opined that technology supports school readiness and impacts success in school.

In another survey, 68% of parents expressed that children are more engaged when educational activities are carried out on tablet devices and 84% believed that tablet devices provide educational benefits to their children (Thiruchelvam, 2014).

Similarly, Vittrup *et.al.* (2014) found that 33% of parents believed young children exposure to electronic gadgets is important for their cognitive development. Additionally, they also believed that "children would fall behind other children academically if their use of technological tools is restricted in early childhood". More than half of the parents who participated in this particular study did not agree that children younger than 2 years old should not be exposed to electronics, despite the recommendations from professionals.

Adamiak (2015) conducted a study on 126 parents of preschoolers and the findings revealed that the majority of parents knew the recommendations of AAP (American Association of Pediatrics) and restricted their children's media viewing to less than the recommended amount. Some parents did not restrict their children's media viewing despite knowing the recommendations. Parent's belief of the impact of television on children's development and parent's use of television as a "babysitter" predicted the amount of television they allowed their children to watch. Adamiak stressed that there is a need for continued education of parents about children's media use recommendations.

Results revealed in a study conducted in 2015 by Lieberman Research Worldwide found that parents approved the growing use of mobile technology in education, and most of them perceived that it improves children's quality of education. Parents also thought that mobile technologies can be especially effective for subjects like math and science (Hill, 2015).

The above studies reveal that majority of parents have positive views towards their children usage of electronic gadgets. Studies with regard to parental monitoring, control and their concerns are presented below.

Nikken and de Haan (2015) conducted a study on 785 parents (children 0-7 years) in the Netherlands. The finding revealed that the parents' experiences of problems when guiding children's digital media use was associated with negative views on media effects, the presence of older siblings living at home and occur especially when their child is active on social media. Parents' feelings of competence were enhanced by positive views on media effects, older children being present in the home, and the involvement of the young child in educational games and media skill level. Parents feel less confident if their child is active on social media. Support is primarily dependent on the level of problems at hand. The study shows that in the absence of older siblings at home, parental concern increases towards the child's activeness on social media and they seek professional help. Parents also seek family or friends suggestions when they have a negative view on media effects.

Marianne (2015) reported in his study that majority of parents prefer to be around their children when using the internet for proper security because young children can be unpredictable in this digital world. Parents even preferred their children to use the internet in the evening when back from school, that is after the necessary domestic activities and their homework is done.

In another research, Nikken (2015) interviewed 896 Dutch parents of 0 to 7 year old children and the results showed that the parents' attitudes about media for children are not strongly associated with the time that children spend on media or with media in the child's bedroom. Parental views on positive and on negative effects of the media are not associated with the time spend on media or the presence of devices in the child's room. The same is true for parents' opinion that media may be too complicated for young children. However, children spend significantly more time with touch screens and have more electronic screens in their bedrooms when their parents agree that the media provide a moment of rest. The results also revealed that mothers more often apply supervision than fathers, and lower educated parents more often use technical restrictions on the child's media use than higher-educated parents. Finally, parents who spend more time on the media themselves are somewhat less inclined to apply active and restrictive mediation on their child's media use.

According to Ofcom report (2017), parents concerns about television content and the time their children spend watching television at home have increased since 2016, with about a fifth of parents of three to four years and a third of parents of five to fifteen years expressed that they have concerns about each of these. There has also been an increase in the proportion of parents who say they are very concerned about what their child has seen on pre-watershed TV, to 6% for 3-4s and 9% for 5-15s, although the majority continues to say they are not concerned.

The studies presented above indicate that the majority of parents have positive perceptions about children usage of electronic gadgets and they expressed that children's use of technology is helpful for their academic performance. Parents did not restrict the usage time in spite of knowing experts recommendations. Some parents prefer to be around their children when using internet due to security reasons.

In a similar way, teachers views about children usage of electronic gadgets are presented in the following section.

PERCEPTIONS OF TEACHERS TOWARDS CHILDREN USAGE OF ELECTRONIC GADGETS

After 'home', next important socializing agent is 'school' for young children. Teachers play a significant role in molding children. Preschool teachers make several decisions in early educational settings, so it is important to give emphasis to teachers' opinions and perceptions.

In a study, Nikolopoulou and Gialamas (2009) mentioned that teachers have positive attitudes and perceptions towards the use and integration of new technologies by young children.

Blackwell *et.al.* (2014) found that early childhood teachers' attitudes towards the role of technology are of great significance in terms of technology use. They mentioned that understanding the current practices, views and beliefs of early childhood teachers towards the use of technology can play a critical role to integrate new technologies since they are the main practitioners in early educational settings.

In a study, 76% of teachers that were surveyed in the UK expressed that tablet devices bring new opportunities to learning that current teaching methods/tools cannot bring (Thiruchelvam, 2014).

Another study conducted by Kara and Cagiltay (2017) examined preschool teachers' thoughts about technology and technology usage in early educational settings. Results revealed that, "7 of 18 preschool teachers agreed that technology helps young children to develop cognitive skills. They also said that technology addresses many senses of children. According to 6 of 18 teachers, technology considers individual differences. The same sample perceived that technology enhances children's psychomotor skills and they also mentioned about improving motivation as an advantage of technology for children. Four of 18 teachers also stated that technology improves hand-eye coordination of children. Besides, 5 teachers emphasized that technology adapts children to future easily. In addition, 5 of 18 teachers pointed out that technology improves the curiosity of children. Three teachers opined that improving self-confidence of children and allowing learning by doing were other advantages of technology for children. Furthermore, rehearsal learning, helping children transfer their knowledge to real life and improving creativity of children were the other advantages of technology for children and only stated by 2 teachers. Eleven of 18 teachers opined that preventing socializing was a disadvantage of technology for children. Five teachers mentioned that technology prevents social play and children spend excessive amount of time while using technology. Four teachers mentioned about psychological problems as one of the disadvantages of technology for children. Additionally, uncontrolled use of technology was another disadvantage of technology for children and stated by 3 teachers. 3 of 18 teachers also stated that technology use can cause health problems for children. Moreover, speech problems and becoming addict were the other disadvantages of technology use for children and stated by 2 teachers as well".

According to NAEYC report (2012), early childhood educators are the decision makers in whether, how, what, when, and why technology and media are implemented through applying their expertise and knowledge of child development and learning, individual children's interests and readiness, and the social and cultural contexts in which children live.

Teachers must constantly make reflective, responsive, and intentional judgments to promote positive outcomes for each child on usage of technology.

There are only few studies available on teachers' perceptions about preschool children usage of technology. The above studies reveal that most of the preschool teachers believe technology usage is beneficial to children. They expressed that usage of gadgets promote children's cognitive development, eye-hand coordination and academic performance.

The review with regard to children usage of technology and their language development, social skills and behaviour problems is presented below.

CHILDREN USAGE OF ELECTRONIC GADGETS AND LANGUAGE DEVELOPMENT

The acquisition of language is one of the most significant achievements of early childhood period. During the early years of life, children learn to master in phonetics, vocabulary of words and grammar. Language is the basis for child's school readiness and achievement.

Christakis (2009) reported that the influence of media on children's language development in the process of first language acquisition, the child spontaneously and gradually develops an ability to use language through interactive situations in his/her natural environment. In addition to the immediate members of the child's family, the child is exposed to language by means of screen media.

There are studies which are evident that children watching interactive and educational content would enhance their language development.

A study revealed that interactive based and narrative based television viewing positively correlated with increased expressive language and vocabulary skills as well as increased emergent literacy skills among children (Linebarger and Walker, 2005).

Linebarger and Walker (2005) found that some particular children's educational shows (e.g. Dora the Explorer and Blue's Clues) had a great positive impact on language production, while Barney and Teletubbies had less influence in children's vocabulary acquisition.

In another study, Zimmerman *et.al.* (2007) found that a small amount of vocabulary was learned when children were exposed to children's education programs, such as Baby Einstein or the Brainy Baby series, for one hour daily. They stressed the notion that children do learn new vocabulary from some interactive children's TV programs.

Linebarger and Piotrowski (2009) saw children's TV programming as the modern storyteller, and they found in their study that exposure to children's TV programs helped children develop and enhance their narrative skills and a sense of chronology in retelling the story. In that skill, they saw an important component of literacy. Further, they noted that the repetition offered in the presentation style formed a link with children acquiring new vocabulary.

Linebarger and Vaala (2010) investigated how screen media affects children's language development by examining the abilities of infants and toddlers to see if they can learn from media. They focused on three factors: (i) attributes of the child (ii) characteristics of screen media stimuli (iii) the varied environmental context surrounding the child's screen media used. They reported that media's effect occurs if the child can identify with its content i.e. it is similar to the child's daily life experiences. Their study also revealed that reading print on the screen developed not only literacy skills but also helped increase children's attention and better comprehension of content.

Thus the studies presented above provided clear evidence that children's educational programs and interactive shows help them to learn new vocabulary, comprehension and expressive language skills.

Some researchers found that parental interactions with children during screen time results in positive impact on their language development.

In a study conducted on 61 toddlers, researchers found that label with voiceover and parental interaction had a positive result in children's imitation and vocabulary learning. Accordingly, label plus voiceover or parental interaction resolved the limitations that exist in child-targeted TV programs (Barr and Wyss 2008).

Mendelsohn *et.al.* (2010) found that verbal interactions (questioning and commenting) between parents and young children have a positive impact on children's language development, and also increases the child's attention to the content on the screen.

Similarly, Bittman *et.al.* (2011) argued that parental participation in tandem with the child's media use is more significant in creating the interactive context and opportunity for using the presented vocabularies in interactive situations to increase the child's linguistic ability. They saw importance in the age-appropriate guided interaction associated with the child's TV exposure habits.

In contrast to the above studies, few researchers have found that children's screen time has increased risk for language development delays.

Kuhl (2004) reported that in studies examining speech-perception learning and speech-production learning, human-human interactions had a strong influence on a child's language development. She also reported that infants learned best from live sessions versus televised ones, and social feedback was an important predictor for the quantity and quality of infant vocalizations. Therefore, heavy television use or excessive screen time can interfere with a child's language development because parents spend less time interacting with and talking to their child. Receptive language delays by age 5 are a significant risk factor for social and emotional problems in adulthood (Schoon *et.al.* 2010).

Duch *et.al.* (2013) study revealed that infants and toddlers who spent more than 2 hours per day watching television had delayed scores in the area of language development when compared with children who were exposed to less than two hours of television per day, whose scores were within typical range for their age.

Results from another study determined that exposure to television was correlated with an increased risk for language developmental delays in young children ages 15 to 35 months old. The exposure group consisted of 75 children who watched an average of 137 minutes in a day. The 75 children in the control group watched an average of 16 minutes in a day. The exposure group's risk of delayed language development was three times higher than that of the control group (Lin *et.al.* 2015).

Roseberry *et.al.* (2009) reported that older children can learn vocabulary from television alone, whereas younger children can learn vocabulary only when supported by social interactions.

In the above studies, researchers examined the association between children screen time and their language development. Most of the studies reveal that there is a positive correlation between language development and screen time of children when children watched age appropriate content and interactive programs. The results also showed delayed language development of children on excessive usage of screen time.

CHILDREN USAGE OF ELECTRONIC GADGETS AND SOCIAL SKILLS

Making friends, sharing, following instructions, expressing emotions are part of socio-emotional development during early childhood. Children must be able to understand the feelings of others, control their own feelings and get along with peers and teachers. Negative early experiences can impair children's mental health and effect their cognitive, behavioural, social-emotional development.

Lanigan *et.al.* (2009) revealed that the computer both supported and impaired family connections. Spending time with computer not only displaces social activities, it also seems to displace other interactive activities like listening to music, reading and family communication. Similarly, the effect of technology time use on children's family relationships might also be moderated by the kind of family activities that may be displaced, content of activities on the technologies, family dynamics and individual characteristics like extroverted or introverted personality.

Straker, *et.al.* (2009) claimed that technology provided both positive and negative impact on social development. The research findings of positive impact on children including "the potential for increased learning opportunities, rapid access to vast stores of information, communication with family and friends, access to an environment where physical attributes or disabilities can be of minimal impact and training of fine motor and visual skills". In addition to positive cognitive and social development, the technology use also had negative impact on children's development, such as (i) child safety (ii) inappropriate cognitive development (exposed to pornography) (iii) inappropriate social development (exposed to aggression and violent content) (iv) displacement of other activities.

In another study, Tran and Subrahmanyam (2013) suggested that the use of technology has a positive impact on children's development in terms of their academic, cognitive and social skills. They proposed three factors through which the use of technologies may influence children's social skills: (i) time on the computer entails time spent on activities relevant to developing social skills and replaces time engaging in other activities relevant to developing social interactions (ii) opportunities for social engagement on the computer can help to develop children's social skills (iii) computer content includes social themes.

Contradicting the above studies, literature with regard to the technology usage of children and negative impact on their social development is presented below.

In a research, results indicated that the moderate use of computers to play games has a negative impact on children's friendships and family relationships, increased use of the internet may be linked to increases in loneliness and depression. Of most concern are the findings that playing violent computer games may increase aggressiveness and diminish a child's ability to distinguish real life from simulation (Subrahmanyam *et.al.* 2000).

Bovill and Livingstone (2001) argued that in the second half of the twentieth century children are spending more and more time in their bedrooms. In recent years a "bedroom culture" has emerged which implies that children and young people are spending "significant proportions of their leisure time at home with the mess media", rather than spending their time in "communal or family space". Bedrooms are now media rich and young people are spending more and more time in their bedrooms for "consumerism and individualization" which is resulting in the "privatization of children's lives". Children and young people are becoming more individualized and socially excluded and as a result, they are spending less time with their family members. It has major influence on social interaction and family communication. There is a negative association "between spending time in the bedroom and spending free time with the family".

Similarly Wellman *et.al.* (2001) argues, when "internet use increases, social contact offline decreases and depression and loneliness increase".

Plowman *et.al.* (2010) establishes three main negative impacts that the technologisation of childhood has resulted in "through television, computers and games consoles". For instance, children's social development is at risk due to increased social isolation as children playing by themselves; their linguistic intellectual and imagination development are at risk. One of the main arguments that Plowman *et.al.* presents that is central to this study is that "opportunities for interactions with family members that promote emotional development are reduced. In other words, new media technologies are having a negative impact on the social interaction between individuals and family members within a household".

Taylor (2012) points out that "technology on its own is neither good nor bad. Any technology a television, computer or phone, for instance is value-neutral. It's how we choose to engage with it that has consequences".

A perusal of the above studies shows that children's usage of technology has both positive and negative impact on their social skills and interactions. They indicate that watching violent content programs result in aggression and violent behaviour among children and increased screen time result in social detachment. On the other hand, studies on positive impact indicate their access to greater information and enhanced communication with family and friends through gadgets.

CHILDREN USAGE OF ELECTRONIC GADGETS AND PROBLEM BEHAVIOUR

Early childhood is a time of rapid growth across all areas of development. Some preschool children show difficult behaviours, identifying and helping these children is a crucial and challenging task. There are many factors associated with childhood behaviour problems such as child's physical health, mental health, socio-economic factors, child rearing practices etc. The findings of researches conducted in the area of impact of children screen time on their behaviour problems are presented below.

Results of Singer and Singer's (1980) study revealed that preschoolers who had behaviour problems in school watched more television than children who did not have behaviour problems in school, these aggressive children also specifically watched more violent action-adventure programs and less pro-social programs.

Data from the National longitudinal survey of youth indicated that TV viewing at age one to three years was associated with parental reports of attention disorder symptoms at age seven. Attention disorder symptoms were indicated by parent response to the five-item hyperactivity subscale of the Behavioural Problems Index (BPI), which assesses concentration, impulsivity, and restlessness. For every additional 2.9 hours of TV viewed per week at age one, a child was 28% more likely to exhibit attention disorder symptoms at age seven (Christakis *et.al.* 2004).

The literature with regard to children usage of electronic gadgets and association with their aggression and violent behaviour is given below.

Friefrich and Stein (2007) investigated TV programming and natural behaviour of pre-school children in Pennsylvania. Ninety three preschool children were shown three types of TV programs each day for 4 weeks. The programs were aggressive cartoons, pro-social programs and neutral films. Results indicated that those children who watched aggressive programs showed more interpersonal aggression than those who saw the neutral programs. There were no effects of television programs on the aggressive behaviour of children who were initially below the median in aggression. There was increased pro-social interpersonal behaviour following exposure to the pro-social program for children who were from low income families.

Daly and Perez (2008) examined whether viewing television violence is associated with aggression in preschool children during spontaneous play in California, USA. They also evaluated simultaneous multiple variables that influence children's behaviour. The target population included 7 preschools with a sample size of 70 children, 32 females and 38 males. Thirty teachers and 26 parents were also interviewed. Results showed that violent TV content was associated with preschool children's aggressive behaviour. Of special significance was that aggression was exacerbated relative to the child's gender.

In another research, Olson *et.al.* (2009) examined 1,254 children to find potential links between problem behaviours and time spent with violent video games. Exposure to mature rated games was a significant predictor of engaging in bullying and aggression, and strongest among girls. The odds of these behaviours increased with the dose of exposure.

Hastings *et.al.* (2009) conducted a study of 70 children ages 6 to 10 via parental report. They sought information concerning the content, amount, and social context (e.g. parental monitoring, with siblings/friends etc.) of children's game playing/computer use and if there is a relationship to child health outcomes. The results of their study were mixed, with the type of media and the amount of time spent with that media largely predictive of positive or negative health outcomes. Educational games provided stress relief, increased attentiveness and school performance. Recreational games were associated with poor school performance and attention, increased aggressiveness, and externalized behaviours. A strong correlation existed between violent video games and aggressive behaviour. He reported that both positive and negative health outcomes more strongly correlated as the time spent in media activity increases. The study also revealed that increased educational media time correlated negatively to behaviour problems (Hastings *et.al.* 2009).

Results from another study found that children's viewing of age-inappropriate content of television programs was related to their aggressive and hyperactive behaviour problems in the classroom. They stressed that it was the content of the television programs rather than the amount of time children spent watching television that had an impact on the development of their social skills (Fussell, 2011).

Thus the above literature reveal that child's screen time is positively associated with attention disorders, impulsivity, restlessness, violent behaviour, aggressiveness and externalized behaviour. So it is important for parents and caretakers to understand the experts' views and recommendations about children's screen time. The literature with regard to experts' recommendations about children usage of electronic gadgets is presented below.

EXPERTS RECOMMENDATIONS ABOUT CHILDREN USAGE OF ELECTRONIC GADGETS

So far the literature cited above is about how children are spending time with gadgets, availability and impact on their development, parents and teachers opinions about usage. It is extremely important to understand practitioners, pediatricians and experts' recommendations on children screen time. The studies presented below show parental control, awareness and experts recommendations.

According to Donohue (2010), early childhood educators need training, opportunities to develop professionally and holistic understanding of technology usage. In recent years smartphones, tablets, game consoles and handheld game devices found their way into the personal and professional lives of early childhood educators and early childhood programs serving young children, parents, and families and into the homes of young children.

Barron *et.al.* (2011) reported that "educators must be knowledgeable and prepared to make informed decisions about how and when to appropriately select, use, integrate, and evaluate technology and media to meet the developmental needs of young children. Educators also need to be knowledgeable enough to answer parents' questions and steer children to technology and media experiences that have the potential to exert a positive influence on their development".

The report of Pearson's National Literacy trust (2014) revealed that, more than 8 in 10 practitioners think that technology is supplemental rather than central to structured activities and free play (85%). Most practitioners have positive views about technology – for example, three quarters of practitioners think it is important to learn to use technology from an early age (75%) and two thirds would like to increase the use of tablet computers in their setting (66%). Practitioners say that a lack of equipment (43%) and financial reasons (38%) are the most common barriers to accessing technology in their setting. Practitioners expressed that irrespective of whether children use a tablet computer with or without an adult, they enjoy using a tablet computer a lot (76%).

Contradicting the above views, Schepper (2011) suggested that for children two and older, caregivers are encouraged to limit screen time to no more than 30 minutes per week during child care, and parents and caregivers are advised to work together to limit children screen time to one to two hours per day.

Similarly, some paediatricians argue that children under two should not be exposed to screen media and children of two and over should only have very limited access to screen time (Sigman, 2012).

In 1999, the American Academy of Paediatrics (AAP) issued a recommendation that children under the age of two watch no television, and for children between the ages of 2 and 3, television viewing be limited. It also recommended that parents limit the amount of time children spend watching television to 1 to 2 hours of quality programs per day. New recommendations in the AAP's Media and Young Minds Brief (2016) suggest that one hour of technology use is appropriate per day, inclusive of time spent at home and in early learning settings and across devices.

Apart from the above studies with regard to experts' recommendations, few researches have also given appropriate strategies and guidelines for parents and educators.

In a study, researchers reported that "considering the profound role of the media on various facets of a child's development, the need of the hour is to find ways to promote the healthy use of the media in the community. This requires the combined efforts of parents, pediatricians, physicians, educators, physicians and policy makers. Physicians, in their role as health promoters, should become more active in sensitizing the media to its impact on youth. Programming decisions should be made with potential consequences to the viewing audience kept in mind. Parental guidance should be available for programmes having violent content. Physicians should make parents and schools "media literate," meaning they should understand the risks of exposure to violence and other inappropriate sexual content. The parents should monitor what programs their children are watching and should also limit the screen time. Children should be guided to interpret and understand on the content they see in television and movies. In doing so, children may be increasingly able to discern which media messages are suitable" (Vivek and Saranya, 2012).

The National Association for the Education of Young Children (NAEYC) and the Fred Rogers Center (2012) state that "appropriate experiences with technology and media allow children to control the medium and the outcome of the experience, to explore the functionality of these tools, and pretend how they might be used in real life". Instead of applying arbitrary, "one-size-fits-all" time limits, families and early educators should determine when and how to use various technol-ogies based on the Three C's: the content, the context, and the needs of the individual child (Guernsey, 2012). They should ask themselves following questions:

Content—How does this help children learn, engage, express, imagine, or explore?

Context—What kinds of social interactions (such as conversations with parents or peers) are happening before, during, and after the use of the technology?

The individual child— Is this technology an appropriate match with this child's needs, abilities, interests, and development stage?

Winpenny *et.al* (2014) suggested that because of strong associations between violent media content and child aggressive behaviour have been clearly documented, parents should continue to monitor the content of their children's media. As many young children own and use electronic devices independently, monitoring and regulation are became difficult tasks for parents. A study from the US that focused on 0-8 year olds found that eighty five percentage of parents set rules on restrictive mediation about times or places technology can be used (Crux Research, 2015).

Hence the above studies indicate that experts recommended screen time for preschoolers should be restricted to one hour per day. There is need for parents to be aware of these recommendations and set time regulations for children.

The review of literature presented above provides clear evidence that gadget usage under age six was found to be almost universal and usage has been increasing year to year. Most of the parents and teachers have positive perceptions on children usage of electronic gadgets. The studies have shown that age appropriate technology can enhance young children's language development. Excessive screen time was positively associated with attention problems, impulsivity, aggression and violent behaviour among children.

Thus the observations made from the available studies helped to conceptualize the problem under investigation.

3

Research Methodology

This chapter illustrates research approach and design considered for the present study. Details of the research design, locale of the study, sample, variables, measurement tools, collection of data, statistical procedures used for the analysis of the data and operational definitions are discussed.

RESEARCH DESIGN

Research design is a plan, structure and strategy of investigation. The present research is aimed to study the "Usage of electronic gadgets among preschool children and their language development, social skills and problem behaviour". The exploratory research design was used for the study. Figure 3.1 shows the research design of the present study.

LOCALE OF THE STUDY

The study was conducted in Hyderabad city, Telangana state because:

- The six electronic gadgets - Television, Smartphone, Computer, Laptop, Tab/IPad and Game console were part of the study. Families having a minimum 4 out of the 6 electronic gadgets were selected by using the purposive sampling technique which will be available in the urban area.
- As the investigator resides at Hyderabad, it is convenient to carry out the work in Hyderabad in terms of time and cost effective.

SAMPLE

Sampling Selection

Initially a survey was conducted to find out total number of private preschools in Hyderabad. There were 1146 private preschools located in Hyderabad.

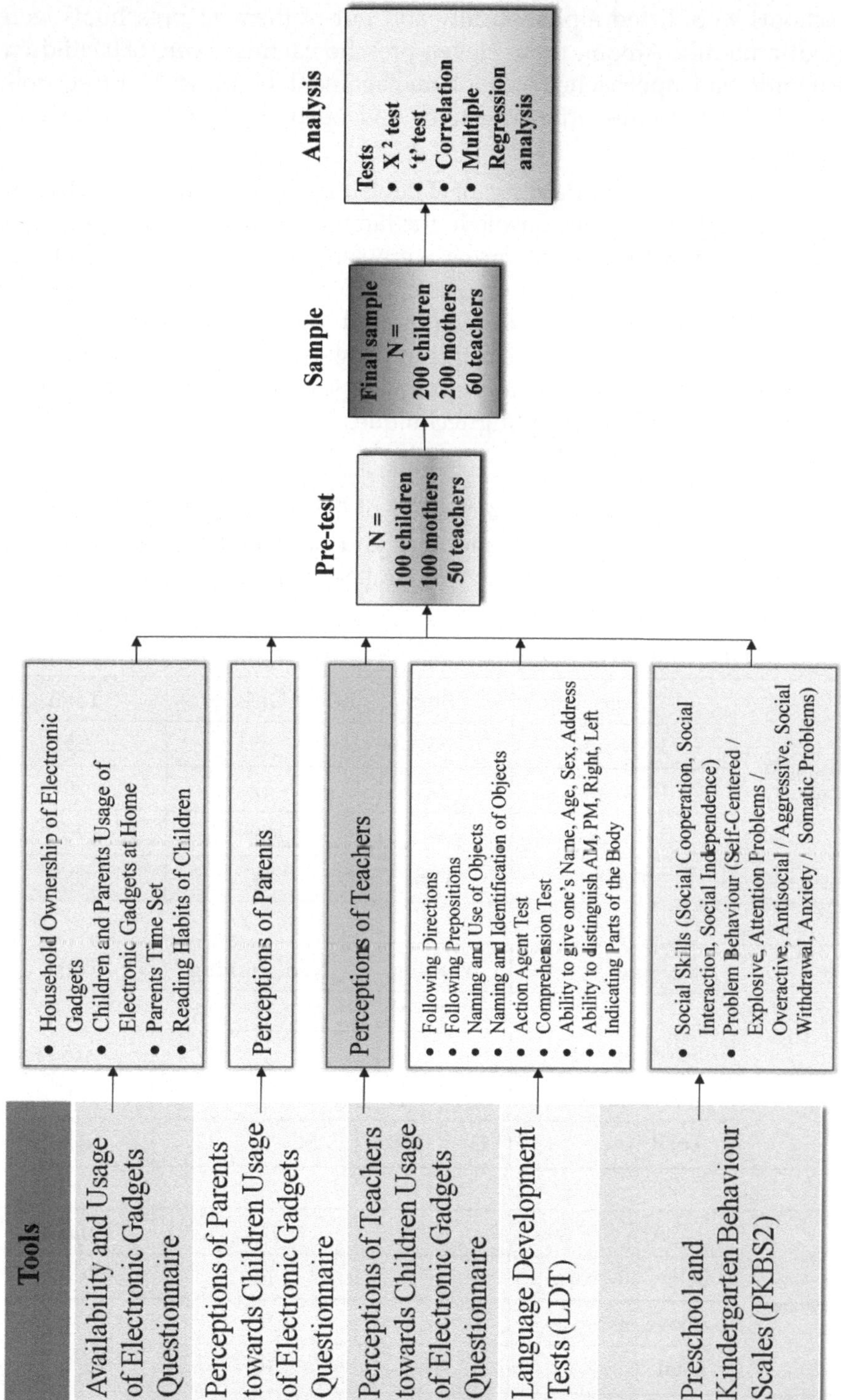

Fig. 3.1: Research Design of the present study

The schools were listed alphabetically and out of them 11 preschools were selected randomly. Among these eleven preschools, there were 680 children. Investigator had approached school management of these 11 preschools, explained about the research objectives and obtained permission for data collection.

To find out the availability of Television, Smart phone, Computer, Laptop, Tablet/Ipad, Game console in the families, a checklist was prepared. Checklists along with consent forms were sent to all 680 parents. Out of 680 parents, 446 given consent to participate in the research. After careful scrutiny of 446 forms, 391 families were found to be suitable for the present study as they have 4 out of 6 electronic gadgets. From these 391 parents, 100 were selected for pre-test and 200 were selected for the final sample by using simple random sampling technique.

Sample

The sample of this study comprised of 200 preschool children in the age group of 3 to 6 years, 200 mothers and 60 preschool teachers from eleven private schools situated in Hyderabad, Telangana State. Table 3.1 shows distribution of the sample.

Table 3.1: Distribution of Sample

	Age	Boys	Girls	Total
Preschool Children	3-4 years	50	35	85
	4-5 years	22	17	39
	5-6 years	47	29	76
	Total	**119**	**81**	**200**

	Age	Working		Non-working		Total
		UG	PG	UG	PG	
Mothers	Below 30 Years	15	14	28	19	76
	Above 30 Years	30	45	26	23	124
	Total	**45**	**59**	**54**	**42**	**200**

	Age	UG	PG	Total
Teachers	Below 30 Years	19	10	29
	Above 30 Years	22	9	31
	Total	**41**	**19**	**60**

VARIABLES AND THEIR EMPIRICAL MEASUREMENTS ARE PRESENTED IN TABLE 3.2

Table 3.2: Variables and their Empirical Measurements

S.No.	Objective	Variables	Tools of Measurement	Analysis
1.	To assess the usage of electronic gadgets among preschool children.	Child's age, gender Parental variables – parents' age, education, occupation Family variables – no. of children, no. of family members, type of family, type of house, availability of play area Reading habits of children	Availability and Usage of Electronic Gadgets Questionnaire	Percentages X^2 test Rank order Regression analysis
2.	To study the perceptions of mothers towards children usage of electronic gadgets.	Mother's age Mother's Education Mother's Working status	Perceptions of Mothers towards Children Usage of Electronic Gadgets Questionnaire	Percentages Rank order 't' values
3.	To study the perceptions of the teachers towards children usage of electronic gadgets.	Teacher's age Teacher's education	Perceptions of Teachers towards Children Usage of Electronic Gadgets Questionnaire	Percentages Rank order 't' values
4.	To compare the language development of low and high electronic gadget usage preschool children.	Child's age, gender Child's usage of electronic gadgets Parent's usage of electronic gadgets	Language Development Tests (LDT)	't' values
5.	To compare the social skills of low and high electronic gadget usage preschool children.	Child's age, gender Child's usage of electronic gadgets Parent's usage of electronic gadgets	Preschool and Kindergarten Behaviour Scales (PKBS2)	X^2 test 't' values Regression analysis
6.	To compare the problem behaviour of low and high electronic gadget usage preschool children.	Child's age, gender Child's usage of electronic gadgets Parent's usage of electronic gadgets	Preschool and Kindergarten Behaviour Scales (PKBS2)	X^2 test 't' values

The sample consists of 119 boys and 81 girls, altogether there are 200 preschool children. Among 200 mothers, 76 mothers belong to below 30 years age group and 124 mothers are in the above 30 years age group. There are 99 undergraduate and 101 postgraduate mothers in the sample. Out of 60 preschool teachers, 29 teachers are below age group of 30 years and 31 belong to above 30 years age group.

MEASUREMENT TOOLS

Availability and Usage of Electronic Gadgets Questionnaire

Description

The items of the schedule were drawn from many sources. The key source for the preparation of the schedule was review of available literature. The questionnaire contains two sections and the first section deals with general profile of the sample. The second section contains 20 questions which include the following aspects:

- Household ownership of electronic gadgets
- Children usage of electronic gadgets during working day and holiday
- Parents usage of electronic gadgets at home
- Child's usage of features and programmes
- Parent's time set
- Availability of resources at home
- Reading habits of children

Initially 15 items were included in the first section (Background Information). In the second section (Availability and usage of electronic gadgets) 20 questions were written. Total numbers of 35 questions were framed for two parts of the schedule. Each of these items was read and evaluated carefully for language, clarity and logical validity.

Experts Evaluation of Items

In order to examine whether given questions were stated clearly, they were arranged in a proper sequence and subjected to experts' scrutiny. The experts were drawn from the fields of education and child development professions. To facilitate the experts in judging the questions, they were requested to indicate:

- Whether the questions clearly stated and easily understood by the participants
- Sequence of the items
- To suggest necessary modifications if any

Based on the experts' suggestions, modifications, additions and elimination of the questions were made. This led to the elimination of

7 items from the initial 35 items. Finally 13 items in first section (Background information of the subjects) and 15 items in the second section (Availability and usage of electronic gadgets), total number of 28 items were included.

Pre-Tryout

The preliminary form of availability and usage of electronic gadgets questionnaire was administered on a sample of 20 parents in order to get the feedback regarding the understandability of questions by the participants. This experience was helpful in making necessary modifications in the language of few items.

Pre-Test

The questionnaire was pre-tested on a sample of 100 mothers of preschool children situated in Hyderabad. Clear instructions were given and the subjects were requested to complete the questionnaire without omitting any item. No time limit was imposed. The responses were carefully scrutinized and scored.

Scoring Procedure

The first section of the schedule has 13 items to elicit the background information of the subjects which is not meant for scoring. The second section consists of 15 items to get information about the usage of electronic gadgets among preschool children. The subjects were asked to give response in five point scale. One to five points were allotted to the options. The highest total score indicates the highest usage of electronic gadgets and lowest score indicates the minimal usage of gadgets.

Psychometric Properties

Reliability

Test re test reliability was calculated by the investigator on a sample of 100 parents with an interval of two weeks. Test re-test reliability of the tool was computed with the gap of two weeks using co-efficient of correlation. The value obtained is 0.88 which was considered reasonably high and reveals that the instrument is suitable to measure the availability and usage of electronic gadgets.

Validity

The validity of any measuring instrument depends upon the accuracy with which it measures and what it intends to measure. All the items were arranged in order and presented to five experts in the field of child development. They were requested to judge the relevance of the items and do necessary required modifications. As per the suggestions given by the experts, some items were reframed and modified.

Perceptions of Mothers towards Children Usage of Electronic Gadgets Questionnaire

Description

In order to design the questionnaire, the available literature was reviewed and information drawn from a variety of sources. On the basis of these sources, statements which are relevant for perceptions of mothers towards children usage of electronic gadgets were framed and the initial form of questionnaire was designed.

The preliminary form of the questionnaire had 35 questions with 2 sections. First section consists of 28 statements to elicit information regarding "perceptions of mothers on children usage of electronic gadgets". The second section contains of 7 questions on "suggestions of mothers regarding usage of electronic gadgets". Each question was carefully evaluated for language, clarity and content.

Experts Evaluation of Items

The questionnaire was subjected for experts' evaluation to see if it can measure perceptions of mothers towards children usage of electronic gadgets and then the questions were arranged in a proper order. They were requested to evaluate whether

(a) the statements clearly stated and easily understood by the participants

(b) order of the statements

(c) to suggest necessary modifications if any

Based on the suggestions given by experts, some statements were modified and rearranged. Each statement was included only when three or more experts agreed upon them and constructed the tool. Four items which are repetitive/not relevant were eliminated out of 35 questions. The final form of the questionnaire contains 31 items. The first section includes 24 statements with 2 point continuum – Agree or Disagree options. The second section consists of 7 questions which include both open-ended and closed-ended.

Pre-Tryout

The questionnaire on mothers' perceptions towards children usage of electronic gadgets was administered on a sample of 20 mothers to get the feedback regarding the understandability of statements by the participants. After this preliminary administration, the ambiguous statements were deleted. The language on few items was changed accordingly.

Pre-Test

After required modifications, the questionnaire was pre-tested on a sample of 100 mothers. Mothers were requested to fill up all the statements without leaving any and no time limit was set. The data was carefully entered and analyzed.

Psychometric Properties

Reliability

The reliability was calculated by the investigator on the sample of 100 mothers with an interval of two weeks. Test re-test reliability of the tool was computed with the gap of 2 weeks. The obtained Spearman-Brown co-efficient reliability is 0.89 which was considered reasonably high.

Split-half method was used to test the internal consistency. The tool was divided into two halves based on the odd and even number of statements. The coefficient of correlation between two sets of scores obtained by Guttman Split-half is 0.73 which indicates high internal consistency of the tool. The Cronbach's Alpha value is 0.79 which indicates that the inter item consistency of the tool is adequately high.

Validity

The statements in the questionnaire were arranged in sequence and presented to the experts and requested to judge the relevance. According to their suggestions, 4 items were eliminated and few items were reconstructed. The final form of the questionnaire consists of 31 questions.

Perceptions of Teachers towards Children Usage of Electronic Gadgets Questionnaire

Description

The tool was prepared to study the teachers' perceptions towards children usage of electronic gadgets. The questions for the schedule were drawn from different sources. The main source for designing the questionnaire is review of literature. Statements which are required to measure were constructed carefully and designed the initial form of the questionnaire.

The preliminary form of questionnaire had 32 questions distributed into 2 sections. The first section contains 24 statements on "perceptions of teachers towards children usage of electronic gadgets" whereas the 8 questions were included to know the "suggestions of teachers about children usage of electronic gadgets". All questions were carefully evaluated for language, clarity and content.

Experts Evaluation of Items

The whole list of statements was submitted to experts who were selected from the field of child development for evaluation purpose. The evaluation sheets included a requesting letter, information about the topic and list of questions. After getting the evaluation forms, the statements were finalized based on their suggestions. Two ambiguous statements were reframed and two repetitive statements were eliminated. Thus the final tool consists of 30 questions – 22 statements on "teachers' perceptions" and 8 questions on "teachers' suggestions".

Pre-Tryout

The preliminary form of the tool was administered on a sample of 20 preschool teachers to know their ease in understanding the statements. This helped in making required modifications in few statements.

Pre-Test

Perceptions of teachers questionnaire was pre-tested on 50 preschool teachers. The subjects were requested to complete the questionnaire without omitting any item and no time limit was imposed. The responses were carefully scrutinized and scored.

Psychometric Properties

Reliability

The test re-test reliability of the tool with gap of two weeks was calculated. The obtained Spearman-Brown co-efficient reliability is 0.86 which indicates that the questionnaire is suitable to measure the perceptions of teachers. To examine the internal consistency of the tool, split-half method was used. The obtained Guttman Split-half value is 0.73 which shows high internal consistency of the tool. The value of Cronbach's Alpha reliability test is 0.67 which states that the inter consistency of the tool is adequately high.

Validity

The validity of any measuring instrument depends upon the accuracy with which it measures and what it intends to measure. In the construction of questionnaire, the questions were selected based on careful analysis of experts. The questions were included under each dimension only when three or more experts agreed upon and the final form of questionnaire includes 30 questions.

Language Development Tests (LDT)

Description

The tests used in this study were taken from NCERT publications (1986). These language tests were adapted from Gesell Scale and modified to the Indian standards. In the present study, few modifications were done by reframing four questions to suit the current trend.

These tests are primarily meant for knowing the degree of understanding the child possesses at different age levels and level of abstraction that the child achieves. The following nine language tests were used for the present study:

1. Following directions
2. Following prepositions
3. Naming and use of objects
4. Naming and identification of objects
5. Action agent test
6. Comprehension test
7. Ability to give one's name, age, sex and address
8. Ability to distinguish right and left
9. Indication of parts of the body

Tests Employed for Language Development

1. **Following Directions:** The purpose of this test was to see the comprehension of instructions given to the child. The complexity of the instruction is increased from the issue of one command to that of two and then to three given simultaneously. The child was asked to follow the directions given to him and act accordingly. This test has 3 items – "Put the ball on the chair", "Pick the books from the table and bring them to me", "Take the ball from the corner, touch the wall and sit down on the chair".

   Scoring

   One mark was assigned for the first item, two marks for the second and three marks for the third. The maximum possible score for the test is 6 and minimum score is 0.

2. **Following Prepositions:** The purpose of the test was to see whether children were able to make distinction among the prepositions and the developmental appraisal of the prepositions. The child was asked to respond according to the instructions given by the instructor. The instructions were given stressing the preposition in the phrase and the object. The prepositions used in this test are – *on, in, behind, under, in-front of, beside*

   Scoring

   One mark was allotted for each direction. The maximum possible score assigned for the test was 6 and minimum score was 0.

3. **Naming and use of objects:** The purpose of the test was to see whether the child will be able to verbalize the name and the comprehension of the 'use' of the object. The responses were analyzed separately for naming as well as for uses. The objects which were given in the original test were – key, paper, knife and bag. As the knife is sharp and harmful for children, instead of knife "spoon" was used in the present study.

   Scoring

   One mark was given for correct naming and one mark for mentioning its use. As the test consists of four objects, the maximum possible score was 8 and minimum score was 0.

4. **Naming and identification of objects:** The purpose of the test is to see the ability to name the picture and in the event of failure to name, to see the ability to recognize the picture. All the items were prepared in picture form cards and each child was asked to name and identify the objects given to him/her. The original tool contains 5 picture cards – rose, needle, cow, book and clock. As most of the children are not seeing the needle now a days, "house" picture was used in the place of needle in the present study.

Scoring

Two marks were allotted for naming of each object and in case of failure to name, one mark was allotted for identification. Since there were five items in the list, the maximum possible score was 10 and minimum score was 0.

5. **Action Agent Test:** This test in additions to providing a measure of language comprehension, the test gives the opportunity to observe such matters as tendencies towards perseveration or stereotype, confusion by similarity of sounds and tendencies to give up easily in the face of an increasingly difficult task. The cards were prepared with pictures of an agent of an action and an irrelevant item drawn on each card, for ex: on a card, a fish and a butterfly drawn and the child had to name the agent that swims.

Scoring

For each action agent item, one mark was allotted. The maximum possible score for the test was 10 and minimum score was 0.

6. **Comprehension Test:** This test is an indicator of higher degree of maturity in developmental scale as the child has to work with some abstract concepts in giving appropriate answers. The child had to give his responses for the questions he/she was asked.

   This test has 4 questions to test the comprehension of children. Among these four questions, one question found to be ambiguous – 'What must one do when one feels hot?' This question is modified as 'What must one do when one breaks his/her toy?'

   Scoring

   Scoring on the level of 'abstraction' as follows:

   - Defeat reaction – when the child accepts his/her inability to answer, ex: don't know
   - Affective reaction – when the response given by the child is emotional, ex: I will cry
   - Specific response – when the response refer to the specific experience of the child, ex: for the question 'what must one do when one is hurt?' the response is 'apply Iodex'
   - Generalized response – the response which is applied to the experience of general group, ex: 'apply medicine'
   - Multiple response – sometimes the child gives more than one response.

   Based on the level of abstraction, no mark for defeat reaction, one mark for the affective, two marks for the specific, three for the generalized and four marks for the multiple responses were assigned for each item. As there are four items, the maximum possible score for the test was 16 and minimum score was 0.

7. **Test showing ability to give one's name, age, sex and address:** The objective of this test was to elicit more information from the child about himself by asking him to give his name, age, sex and address.

   This test has 5 questions – What is your name? What is your father's name? How old are you? Are you a boy or girl? Where do you live? The fifth question "where do you live" is generic and creates confusion in the subjects. The question was changed as "In which city do you live".

   Scoring

   One mark was assigned for each item. As there were five items in the test, the maximum possible score was 5 and minimum score was 0.

8. **Test showing ability to distinguish A.M., P.M., Right and Left:** The investigator secured the child's attention and then asked questions in a casual manner to test his ability to distinguish between A.M., P.M., Right and Left. This test is designed to see the development of the concepts of 'right' and 'left' in the child.

   Scoring

   For each correct response one mark to be given. The maximum possible score for the test is 5 and minimum was 0.

9. **Indication of parts of the body:** The child was asked to indicate various parts of his body following the instructions given to him/her by the investigator. Nine body parts were included in this test – *ears, tongue, thumb, palm, hair, nail, knees, cheek* and *chin.*

   Scoring

   One mark was assigned for each item. As there were five items in the test, the maximum possible score was 9 and minimum score was 0.

   Among the 9 language tests, four questions were modified and reframed and the modified version of tool was ready for pre-tryout.

Pre-Tryout

The language development test was administered on a sample of 20 preschool children to check the understandability of instructions by the students. After careful observations from pre try-out, the tests were further modified with more clarity of instructions.

Pre-Test

The language development test was pre-tested on a sample of 100 preschool students the data was carefully scrutinized and scored.

Scoring Procedure

The tool contains 9 language tests aimed to study the language development of preschool children. Each test has subtests and marks were allotted for 51 subtests as per the instructions of the tool. The highest possible score is 75 and least possible score is 0. Highest score indicates the higher language development of children.

Psychometric Properties

Reliability

A reliability analysis was carried out on the Language development scale comprising 9 tests. Cronbach's alpha is 0.857, which indicates a high level of internal consistency for the scale. Most items appeared to be worthy of retention, resulting in a decrease in the alpha if deleted. Thus it reveals that the instrument is suitable to measure the language development of children. Cronbach alpha reliability of each language test is given below.

S.No.	Language Development Test	Cronbach's Alpha Reliability
1.	Following directions	.840
2.	Following prepositions	.845
3.	Naming and identification of objects	.845
4.	Naming and use of objects	.840
5.	Action agent test	.819
6.	Comprehension test	.885
7.	Ability to give one's name, age, sex and address	.839
8.	Ability to distinguish right and left	.840
9.	Indication of parts of the body	.837

Validity

All the items in the tool have significant correlation with each other at 0.01 level (2-tailed) and also to the total, hence all the items are valid and they measure what it has to measure.

Preschool and Kindergarten Behaviour Scales (PKBS2)

Description

Preschool and Kindergarten Behaviour Scales – Second Edition (PKBS-2) is a behavioural rating instrument for the use in evaluating social skills and problem behaviour patterns of preschool and kindergarten aged children, aged three through six. It is a norm referenced, standardized instrument developed by Merrell (2002) specifically for use in assessing young children in a variety of settings and by a variety of behavioural informants. The PKBS2 includes two major scales: *Social skills* (34 items) and *Problem behaviour* (42 items).

Scale A: Social Skills: The Social Skills scale includes 34 items that describe adaptive or positive behaviours that are likely to lead to positive personal and social outcomes. These items are rated on a 4-point scale where the anchor points are as follows: 0 = Never, 1 = Rarely, 2 = Sometimes and 3 = Often. The items within scale A are divided into three empirically derived subscales: Subscale Al, *Social Cooperation,* includes 12 items that reflect behaviours and characteristics deemed important in following instructions from adults, cooperating and compromising with peers, and showing appropriate self- restraint. Subscale A2, *Social Interaction,* includes 11 items that reflect behaviours and characteristics deemed important in gaining and maintaining acceptance and friendship from others. Subscale A3, *Social Independence,* includes 11 items that reflect behaviours and characteristics deemed important in achieving social independence within the domain of the peer group.

Scale B: Problem Behaviour: The Problem Behaviour scale includes 42 items that describe various problem behaviours commonly seen in the early childhood/preschool population. These items are rated on the same 4-point scale previously described for Scale A. The Problem Behaviour scale measure both externalising and internalising social-emotional problems on five subscales: Self-Centered/Explosive, Attention Problems/Overactive, Antisocial/Aggressive, Social Withdrawal, and Anxiety/Somatic Problems.

Scoring Procedure

The items are rated on a scale from 0 to 3 (0 being "never", and 3 being "often"). Scoring the PKBS is relatively simple, straightforward and involves two steps: 1. Calculating raw scores for the subscale and total scores. 2. Converting raw scores to standard scores, percentile ranks, and functional levels using the raw score conversion table.

Psychometric Properties

Reliability

The original form of PKBS has been shown to have adequate to excellent psychometric properties. Internal consistency coefficients have all been in the .90 range. Internal consistency of the social skills and problem behaviour total scores of the PKBS was estimated using Cronbach's alpha coefficient method. The resulting internal consistency reliability coefficients were .87 for the social skills items (scale A), and .92 for the problem behaviour items (scale B). In terms of the representativeness of the standardization sample used for norming the PKBS2, the nationwide sample included 3,313 preschool and kindergarten students, ages 3 through 6, which reflected the ethnicity, socioeconomic status, and special education classification similar to those characteristics of the US population according to the 2000 U.S. Census.

For the present study, Cronbach's alpha was calculated on 100 sample for norming the reliability suitable to Indian standards. The obtained value is .96 for social scale and .94 for problem behaviour scale which shows high internal consistency of the tool.

Validity

For the original tool, Bivariate Pearson product-moment correlations were calculated between individual items and their respective total scale scores to examine the extent to which items fit within their domain. For the Social Skills Scale, most items correlated in the 0.60 to 0.70 range, with five items in the 0.52 to 0.59 range, three items in the 0.44 to 0.49 range and one item at 0.32. For the Problem Behaviour Scale, items were relatively evenly distributed between 0.4 and 0.75.

In the present study, all the items in PKBS scale have significant correlation with each other at 0.01 level (2-tailed) and also to the total, hence it indicates that all the items are valid and they measure what it has to measure.

DATA COLLECTION

In the first step, prior information was given to mothers about data collection and requested them to gather in the school premises at a given time. Clear instructions were given to the mothers and they were seated separately to avoid discussions. The data was collected in one session with an interval of 10 minutes between two questionnaires. No time limit was imposed for completing the questionnaires. 'Availability and usage of electronic gadgets questionnaire' was given first and mothers took approximately 20-30 minutes for completion. After 10 minutes gap, 'perceptions of mothers towards children usage of gadgets questionnaires' were given to mothers. They consumed around 45 minutes to fill up the questionnaires.

Preschool teachers were available after school working hours. They were seated separately to avoid discussions. In one session, 'Perceptions of teachers towards children usage of electronic gadgets questionnaire' was given and it took nearly 45 minutes for them to fill the questionnaire. For the second session, teachers who were handling selected preschool children for the final sample were gathered to complete the PKBS2 tool. 'Preschool and Kindergarten Behaviour Scale' was given to those class teachers and approximately they took one hour to complete the tool. Each teacher could complete 5-6 forms per session.

Language development tests were administered individually on preschool children. Each child was called into a separate room and built rapport with them before administering the test. After establishing good rapport with children, nine language tests were administered on individual children with the help of class teachers and results were recorded carefully. On each working day during school hours, investigator could assess 8-10 children. Children enjoyed doing these language tests.

Depending on the requirement, the investigator had to visit each preschool for 4 to 5 times for the completion of data. Then the collected data was computed for statistical analysis.

STATISTICAL ANALYSIS

The statistical tests used in the present study are

- Chi-square test
- 't' test
- Correlation test
- Regression analysis

OPERATIONAL DEFINITIONS

Electronic Gadget

A gadget that accomplishes its purpose electronically. The present study includes six electronic gadgets – Television, Smart Phone, Computer, Laptop, Tablet/IPad and Game console.

Preschool Age

Preschool or an early childhood centre is a broad term which is used to describe an educational centre that serves approximately 3-6 years age group children. The present study confined to 3 to 6 years age group children.

Language Development

Language development is a higher level cognitive skill involving audition and oral abilities in humans to communicate verbally individuals' wants and needs (Rudd and Kelley, 2011).

The present study deals with 9 language aspects – following directions, following prepositions, naming and identification of objects, naming and use of objects, action agent test, comprehension test, ability to give one's name, age, sex and address, ability to distinguish right and left and indication of parts of the body.

Social Skills

Social skills can be defined as the set of skills people use to interact and communicate with one another. They are based on the social norms of our society and they tell us what attitudes and behaviours are considered to be normal, acceptable and expected in a particular social situation (Patrick, 2008).

In the present study, 3 specific social skill elements were selected – social cooperation, social interaction and social independence.

Problem Behaviour

Problem behaviour theory defines *problem behaviour* as anything that can interfere with successful psychosocial development and *problem behaviour* as risk behaviours that elicit either formal or informal social responses designed to control them (Jessor and Jessor, 1977).

The present study is confined to the following problem behaviour traits: Self-centered, explosive, attention problems, overactive, antisocial, aggressive, social withdrawal, anxiety and somatic problems.

4

Results and Discussion

This chapter deals with the findings of the study. The main objective of the present research is to study the usage of electronic gadgets among preschool children, their language development, social skills and behaviour problems.

PRESCHOOL CHILDREN USAGE OF ELECTRONIC GADGETS

This section further classified into two parts – background information of the subjects and usage of electronic gadgets.

Background Information of Subjects

The sample of this study comprised of 200 children between 3 to 6 years old age group, 200 mothers and 60 preschool teachers. Table 4.1 depicts the general profile of preschool children.

Table 4.1: General Profile of Children (N=200)

S.No.	Category	Number	Percentage
(1)	(2)	(3)	(4)
1.	**Gender**		
	Boys	119	59.5
	Girls	81	40.5
2.	**Age**		
	3-4 years	85	42.5
	4-5 years	39	19.5
	5-6 years	76	38.0
3.	**Number of children**		
	Single child	109	54.5
	2 children	91	45.5

(Table Contd...)

(1)	(2)	(3)	(4)
4.	**Type of Family**		
	Nuclear	147	73.5
	Extended	53	26.5
5.	**Type of House**		
	Apartment	118	59.0
	Independent	82	41.0
6.	**Availability of Play Area**		
	Not available	39	19.5
	Available	161	80.5

It is observed from the table that there are about 60 percent of boys and 40 percent of girls in the sample. Forty two percent of children belong to 3-4 years, nineteen percent are in the 4-5 year old age group and thirty eight percent are in the 5-6 years age group.

The above table shows that 55% of families are having single child and 45% percent families have two children. Nearly three fourth (73%) of families are nuclear and one fourth (26%) are extended families. The data reveals that fifty nine percent of families are living in the apartments while forty one percent are living in the independent houses. Majority of the families (80%) are having enough space for children to play and 20% of the houses do not have play area. Hence the data indicates that majority of the families are nuclear with single child and live in apartments. General information about the parents is presented in table 4.2.

Table 4.2: General Profile of Parents

S.No.	Category	Mothers (N=200) N (%)	Fathers (N=200) N (%)
1.	**Age**		
	25-29 years	76 (38.0)	12 (6.0)
	30-34 years	93 (46.5)	73 (36.5)
	35-39 years	26 (13.0)	94 (47.0)
	40-44 years	5 (2.5)	21 (10.5)
2.	**Education**		
	UG	99 (49.5)	52 (26.0)
	PG	101 (50.5)	148 (74.0)
3.	**Occupation**		
	Govt. job	9 (4.5)	21 (10.5)
	Pvt. Job	89 (44.5)	146 (73.0)
	Business	6 (3.0)	33 (16.5)
	Homemaker	96 (48.0)	0 (0)

It is noticed from the above table that nearly half (46.5) of the mothers belong to 30-34 year old age group, whereas around half (47%) of fathers belong to 35-39 year old age group. This is followed by 38% of the mothers who are in between 25 and 29 years age and 36.5% of fathers are between 30 and 34 years age.

Around half (49.5%) of mothers and one fourth (26%) of fathers are graduates. Nearly fifty one (50.5%) of mothers are postgraduates whereas around three fourth (76%) fathers are post graduates.

About 4.5% of mothers and 10.5% of fathers are government jobholders. Around half (44.5%) of mothers and three fourth (73%) of fathers are working in private organizations. Three percent of mothers and 16.5% of fathers are doing business. Forty eight percent of mothers are homemakers whereas all fathers are working.

Thus majority of the parents of selected preschool children are in the age group of 30s and are working in private organizations in the twin cities of Hyderabad. Background information of the teachers is presented in table 4.3.

Table 4.3: General Profile of Teachers (N=60)

S.No.	Category	Number	Percentage
1.	**Age**		
	< 30 years	29	48.3
	> 30 years	31	51.7
2.	**Education**		
	UG	41	68.3
	PG	19	31.7
3.	**Designation**		
	UKG teacher	15	25.0
	LKG teacher	17	28.3
	Nursery teacher	19	31.7
	Playgroup teacher	9	15.0

Forty eight percent of teachers are under the age group of 30 years and 52% of them belong to above 30 years age. Sixty eight teachers are under graduates and 32% of them did their post graduation. Thirty two percent of sample are Nursery teachers, followed by 28% are LKG teachers, 25% are UKG teachers and 15% are Playgroup teachers.

Preschool Children Usage of Electronic Gadgets

The data collected on various aspects like availability of the gadgets, number of gadgets available, ownership of the gadget by the child and internet connection are presented in table 4.4.

Table 4.4: Household Ownership of Electronic Gadgets (N=200)

Electronic Gadgets	Availability				Internet/Satellite Connection		Whether Child Owned the Gadget	
	One Set	More than One Set	Total	Not available	Yes N (%)	No N (%)	Yes N (%)	No N (%)
Television	170 (85.0)	28 (15.0)	198 (99.0)	2 (1.0)	177 (88.5)	23 (11.5)	1 (0.5)	199 (99.5)
Smartphone	26 (13.0)	173 (86.5)	199 (99.5)	1 (0.5)	190 (95.0)	10 (5.0)	3 (2.5)	197 (98.5)
Computer	104 (52.0)	5 (2.5)	109 (54.5)	91 (45.5)	93 (46.5)	107 (53.5)	5 (2.5)	195 (97.5)
Laptop	113 (56.5)	41 (20.5)	154 (77.0)	46 (23.0)	141 (70.5)	59 (29.5)	2 (1.0)	198 (99.0)
Tablet/IPad	81 (40.5)	21 (10.5)	102 (51.0)	98 (49.0)	97 (48.5)	103 (51.5)	47 (23.5)	153 (76.5)
Game Console	34 (17.0)	0 (0)	34 (17.0)	166 (83.0)	34 (17.0)	166 (83.0)	20 (10.0)	180 (90.0)

Digital screens have become an inseparable part of our lives. Almost all families (99%) are having television set with satellite connection (88.5%) at home. Fifteen percent of them are having more than one television set. In the same way, all families (99.5%) are having smartphones except one who is using basic model mobile. Majority (86.5%) of them are having more than one smart phone at home with internet facility (95%). More than half (54.5%) of the families have computers with internet connection (46.5%) and only 2.5% families have more than one computer set at home. Seventy seven percent of the families are having laptops with internet facility (70.5%) and 20.5% of them are having more than one laptop. Nearly half (51%) of the families have tablets with internet connection (48.5%). Among them, 10.5% of the families are having more than one tablet/IPad. Seventeen percent of the families are having one set of game console with internet connection.

Similar results were observed in the Ofcom (2017) report, that showed more preschool children are online than in 2016, with increase of more than ten percent and more than half (53%) of 3 to 4 years and 79% of 5 to 7 years are online.

Studies have shown that parents are purchasing electronic gadgets for children in the preschool age itself. Rhodes (2017) surveyed 651 three to six year old children in Australia and the findings revealed that 36% of them have their own tablet and/or smartphones.

In the present study also 23.5% of preschool children are having their own tablet/IPad and 10% are owned game consoles. Some parents have expressed that they are gifting the gadgets to their kids on the occasions like their birthdays, festivals etc.

These results are in line with the Ofcom (2017) survey which revealed that, 21% of 3 to 4 year children and 35% of 5 to 7 year old children have their own tablet. One percent of 3 to 4 year children and 5% of 5 to 7 year old children owned smart phone.

To study the usage of different electronic gadgets – television, smart phone, computer, laptop, tablet, IPad and game console by children and parents, an attempt is made to classify the subject scores into three categories as low, average and high based on the mean and SD value of obtained raw scores. The higher score indicates the higher usage of gadgets. The below table represents the association between child's usage of electronic gadgets on working day and holiday.

Table 4.5: Association between Child's Usage of Electronic Gadgets on a Typical Working Day and Holiday (N=200)

Score	Working Day N (%)	Holiday N (%)	X^2 test
Low (Below 9)	95 (47.5)	58 (29.0)	21.19***
Average (10 to 11)	65 (32.5)	64 (32.0)	
High (Above 12)	40 (20.0)	78 (39.0)	

The results reveal from the above table that usage of electronic gadgets is high in 20% of preschool children during working day whereas it is almost doubled (39%) during holiday. Usage is low in 47.5% of children on a working day while it is low in 29% of children during holiday.

The obtained chi-square value of usage of electronic gadgets by the child on working day and holiday is 21.19 which is more than the table value at 0.01 level. Hence it is found that preschool children are spending more time with gadgets on holidays than working days. Figure 4.1 depicts the children's usage of electronic gadgets on a typical working day and holiday.

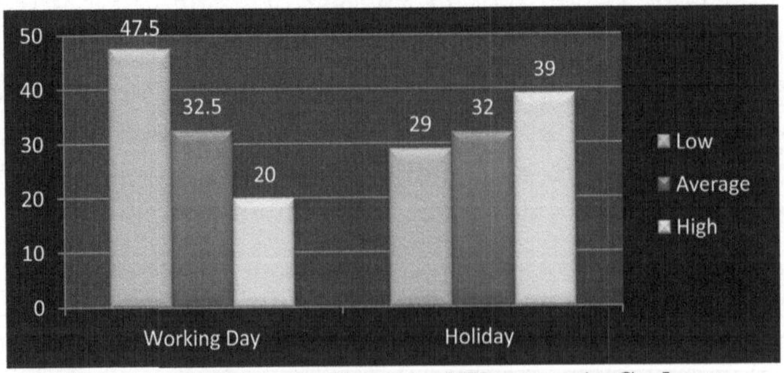

Fig. 4.1: Children's Usage of Electronic Gadgets on a Typical Working Day and Holiday

It can be observed from the above figure that children usage of gadgets is more during holiday compared to working day. The results are similar with findings of Ofcom report (2017) which showed that young children are spending online for one hour, playing video games for 48 minutes and watching television for 2 hours on a typical working day. Whereas they are spending more time during holidays – online 1 hour 24 minutes, video games 1 hour 12 minutes and watching television for 2 hours 36 minutes.

If parents engage children with constructive activities like art and craft, board games, puzzles etc, they can divert children from the gadgets and reduce screen time. To understand the association between age and children usage of electronic gadgets, chi-square values were calculated and the results presented below.

Table 4.6: Association between Age and Usage of Electronic Gadgets on a Typical Working Day and Holiday (N=200)

Score	3 to 4 years (N=85)	4 to 5 years (N=39)	5 to 6 years (N=76)	X^2 test
	N (%)	N (%)	N (%)	
Working Day				
Low (Below 9)	43 (50)	17 (43)	35 (46)	
Average (10 to 11)	27 (32)	14 (36)	23 (30)	1.30 @
High (Above 12)	15 (18)	8 (21)	18 (24)	
Holiday				
Low (Below 9)	32 (38)	24 (28)	29 (34)	
Average (10 to 11)	11 (28)	19 (49)	9 (23)	15.36*
High (Above 12)	15 (20)	21 (28)	40 (53)	

* Significant at 0.05 level

@ Not Significant

The above table shows that there is no association between age and usage of electronic gadgets on a typical working day. In contrast, significant association found between age and usage of gadgets during holiday. The obtained chi-square value is 15.36 which is more than the table value at 0.05 level. Thus it can be observed that when the age increases, children usage of electronic gadgets on holiday has been increased significantly. The figure 4.2 shows the usage of electronic gadgets among 3 to 4 years, 4 to 5 years and 5 to 6year old children on a typical working day.

It can be seen from the figure 4.2 that there is gradual increase in the gadget usage when children age increases. Children usage of electronic gadgets during holiday is higher than the usage on a typical working day.

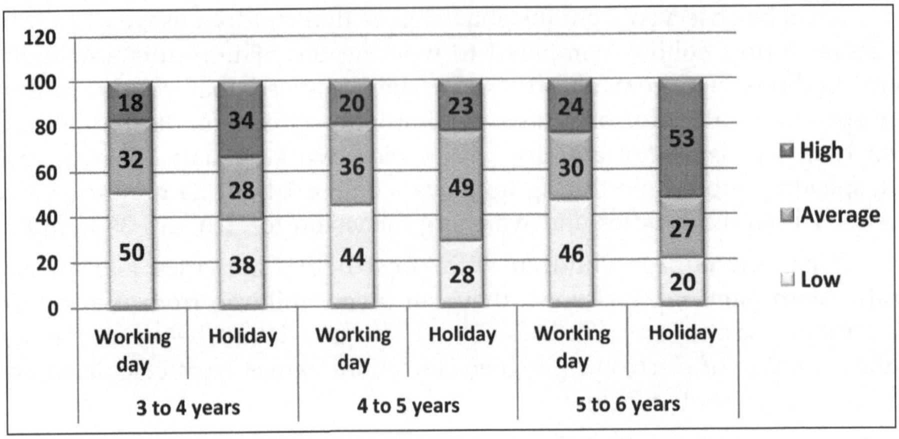

Fig. 4.2: Usage of Electronic Gadgets among 3-4, 4-5 and 5-6 year Old Children on a Typical Working Day

The Null Hypothesis Stated: *"Age has no effect on usage of electronic gadgets among preschool children"*. Based on the results of the present study, the null hypothesis could be partially accepted. No significant association was found between age and usage of electronic gadgets during working day whereas significant association was found between age and usage of electronic gadgets on a holiday.

Gender is found to be one of the factors which influence usage of time and studies have shown gender variations in usage of electronic gadgets. Barr-Anderson etal, (2011) found that boys' screen time was half an hour more than the girls' screen time in a day. Table 4.7 shows the association between gender and usage of gadgets on a working day and holiday.

Table 4.7: Association between Gender and Usage of Electronic Gadgets on a Typical Working Day and Holiday (Boys N=119 and Girls N=81)

Usage time	Gender	Low	Average	High	X^2 test
Working Day	**Boys**	54 (45)	39 (33)	26 (22)	0.50 @
	Girls	41 (50)	24 (30)	16 (20)	
Holiday	**Boys**	34 (29)	31 (26)	54 (45)	6.37*
	Girls	24 (30)	33 (40)	24 (30)	

* Significant at 0.05 level

@ Not Significant

The findings of the above table show that usage of electronic gadgets is high in 22% boys and 20% of girls on a typical working day. Whereas usage is high in 45% of boys and 30% of girls on a holiday. Chi square value 0.50 showed that there is no association between gender and usage of electronic gadgets on a typical working day.

The obtained chi-square value of boys and girls usage of electronic gadgets on a holiday is 6.37 which is more than table value at 0.05 level. Thus it reveals that boys are spending more time with gadgets on a holiday as compared to girls. Some parents have opined that it is easy to control girls than boys when they set timings and also expressed that boys throw tantrums. Figure 4.3 represents the distribution of boys and girls usage of gadgets on working day and holiday.

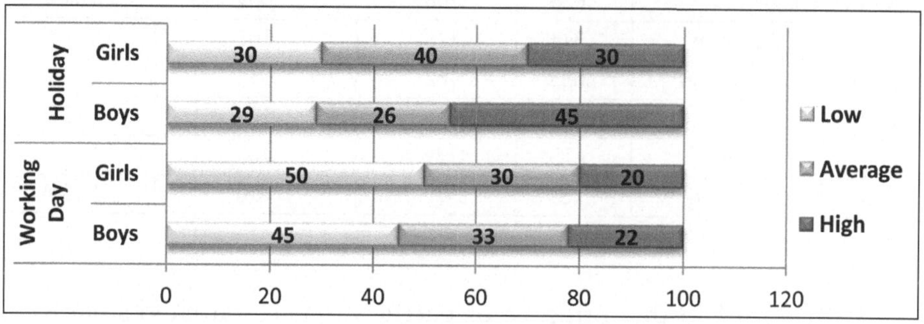

Fig. 4.3: Level of Usage of Electronic Gadgets by Boys and Girls on a Typical Working Day and Holiday

These results are consistent with the findings of O'Neill *et.al* (2005) research which revealed that internet usage is slightly higher in boys compared with girls. More than half (51%) of boys and 48% of girls were using internet in their sample. Boys were more likely (nearly 21%) to use the internet than girls (over 18%) and boys seem to be more proactive, or interested, in using the Internet. Their data also revealed that boys report greater levels of access to games consoles compared with girls.

The Null Hypothesis Stated: *"Preschool boys and girls do not differ on the usage of electronic gadgets"*. In the present study, null hypothesis could be partially accepted as no significant association was found between boys and girls on a typical working day while significant association was found between boys and girls during holiday.

There are many factors which influences children's usage of electronic devices. Different factors regression analysis is carried out treating child's usage of electronic gadgets as dependent variable and mother's education, occupation, father's age, education and occupation as independent variables and the results are presented in the below table 4.8.

Table 4.8: Influence of Parental Variables on Child's Usage of Electronic Gadgets on a Typical Working Day

Coefficients				
Model	Unstandardized Coefficients		Standardized Coefficients	't' value
	B	Std. Error	Beta	
Mother's age	.028	.308	.009	0.09@
Mother's education	.344	.176	.161	1.96*
Mother's occupation	.085	.162	.038	0.53@
Father's age	.376	.266	.134	1.41@
Father's education	.175	.129	.105	1.36@
Father's occupation	.368	.320	.090	1.15@

* Significant at 0.05 level
@ Not Significant

With regard to the influence of parent variables on child's electronic gadget usage, the above table indicates that mother's education has significant impact on child's usage of electronic gadgets at 0.05 level of significance. Other variables like mother's age, occupation, father's age, education and occupation do not significantly affect the child's usage of electronic devices. Thus it is evident that mother's education creates an impact on child's usage of gadgets as mothers spend most of the time with preschool children and educated mothers can monitor the content and regulate timings.

Apart from parental factors, to study the influence of family variables, regression analysis is carried out treating child's usage of electronic gadgets as dependent variable and number of children, number of family members, type of family, type of house, play area as independent variables and the findings are presented in table 4.9.

Table 4.9: Influence of Family Variables on Child's Usage of Electronic Gadgets on a Typical Working Day

Coefficients				
Model	Unstandardized Coefficients		Standardized Coefficients	't' value
	B	Std. Error	Beta	
No. of children	.403	.337	.096	1.19@
No. of family members	.124	.171	.080	0.72@
Type of family	.025	.276	.009	0.09@
Type of house	.028	.353	.006	0.08@
Play area	.837	.425	.140	1.97*

* Significant at 0.05 level
@ Not Significant

With regard to the influence of family variables on child's electronic gadget usage, the above table indicates that play area at home has significant impact on child's usage of electronic gadgets at 0.05 level of significance. Other variables like number of children, family members, type of family, type of house do not significantly affect the child's usage of electronic devices. When children have sufficient play area at home, they get opportunity in playing games instead of spending time with gadgets.

As parents are role models to children and they imitate parents in the preschool stage, parental usage of electronic gadgets may influence children's usage. A study conducted by Erikson's institute (2016) on thousand preschool children found that 16% of their parents' screen time is more than 2 hours per day, 23% spend 1-2 hours, 35% spend 30-60 minutes, 21% spend less than half an hour and 6% of parents do not spend time with gadgets.

Findings of an Indian research revealed that 323 (71.7%) parents used mobile for 1-3 hours and 61 (13.5%) parents were using mobiles for more than 4 hours per day (Bansal and Mahajan, 2017). In the present study, mothers' and fathers' usage of electronic gadgets is presented in table 4.10.

Table 4.10: Association between Mothers' Usage and Fathers' Usage of Electronic Gadgets on a Typical Working Day

Score	Mother's Usage (N=200)	Father's Usage (N=200)	X^2 test
	N (%)	N (%)	
Low (Below 9)	71 (35.5)	45 (22.5)	14.75**
Average (10 to 11)	73 (36.5)	64 (32.0)	
High (Above 12)	56 (28.0)	91 (45.5)	

** Significant at 0.01 level

The above table shows that 28% of mothers scored high in the usage of electronic gadgets whereas 45.5% of fathers scored high in the usage on a working day. The obtained chi-square value of usage of electronic gadgets by mother and father is 14.75 which is more than table value at 0.01 level. Thus it is revealed that fathers are spending more time with electronic gadgets when compared with mothers.

Figure 4.4 represents usage of electronic gadgets on a typical working day by mothers and fathers.

In general, preschool children spend most of the time with mothers when compared with fathers. Due to more responsibilities like household tasks, child rearing and jobs mothers spend less time with electronic gadgets compared with fathers.

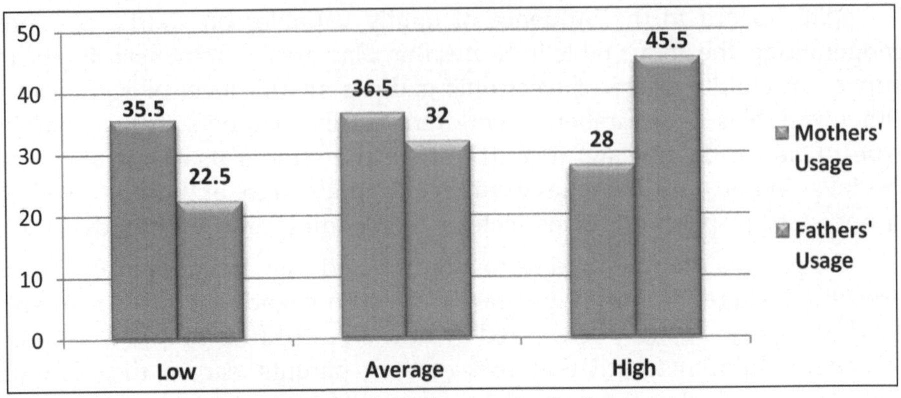

Fig. 4.4: Usage of Electronic Gadgets on a Typical Working Day by Mothers and Fathers

In day today life, we can observe young children are using gadgets at various timings like while having their meal, after school hours, bed time etc. To know how children are using gadgets at specific timings – before going to school, after reaching home, meal time and bed time the data collected and presented in the following table 4.11.

Table 4.11: Child's Usage of Electronic Gadgets during Particular Time on a Working Day (N=200)

Time of usage	Number	Percentage
a (before going to school)	4	2.0
b (after reaching home)	33	16.5
c (meal time)	42	21.0
d (before bed time)	20	10.0
e (do not use)	5	2.5
b, c	23	11.5
b, d	20	10.0
a, b, c	14	7.0
b, c, d	20	10.0
a, b, c, d	19	9.5

Based on the parents' response, different combinations of answers were analyzed. The results reveal that 21% of preschool children are using gadgets during meal time, 16.5% are using after reaching home from school and 10% of them are using before bed time. Eleven percent of children are using the gadgets twice in a day i.e. after reaching home and meal time and similarly 10% are using after reaching home and before bed time.

Seventeen percent of children are using gadgets thrice in a day – 7% are using before going to school, after reaching home and meal time where as 10% of them are using after reaching home from school, meal time and before bed time. The findings also show that 10% of children are using the gadgets throughout the day – before going to school, after reaching home, meal time and bed time.

Hence it is observed from the results that most of the preschool children are using gadgets during meal time and mothers have expressed that it helps to make them complete their meal faster.

The data also demonstrates that children are using gadgets more often after school hours. These results were consistent with the findings of Barr-Anderson (2011) study that children watching television after school (12.9%) was more than twice as common as watching television before school (4.5%).

In order to know operating features and programs used by children in the electronic gadgets, the data was arranged in rank order based on the obtained total scores. The least possible score is 200 and highest possible score is 600 for each option and the results are presented in the table 4.12.

Table 4.12: Features and Programs Used by the Child (N=200)

	Total Score	Rank Order
Features		
Games	424	1
Video	404	2
Internet	394	3
Camera	384	4
Music	370	5
Programmes		
Cartoons	518	1
Educational programmes	425	2
Videos	400	3
Games	383	4
Music	354	5

It is noticed from the above table that majority of children are operating game apps in the gadgets, followed by videos, internet, camera and music features. Some parents have mentioned that children are using the popular apps like *bubble shoot, temple run, talking tom, candy crush, Pokémon go etc.*

Table 4.12 also indicates that a greater part of children are watching cartoons in the gadgets followed by educational programs, videos, games and music. Parents reported that their children are watching nursery rhymes and stories in the *YouTube videos*, watching cartoon channels like *Doraemon, Tom and Jerry, Sesame Street, Chota Bheem, Motu Patlu, Roll No.21, Sponge Bob, Pokémon, Oggy and Cockroaches etc.*

Thus it is evident that the present generation children have access to various gadgets at home and also are adapt at using touch screens with ease.

Similar results were found in a study conducted by Given *et.al* (2014) on how children engaged in various technology related activities while using their devices. Children tapped the IPad screen while using an application, watched YouTube videos, looked at family photos, created digital artwork and listened to music. The most common technology related activity was watching or listening to something on the computer screen (23%) and thirteen percent of children responded by jumping or squealing in response to what was on the screen. Playing a game on the device (15%) was also popular and comprised the next largest category of computer use. The children also spent time waiting for programs to load (5%) or selecting an option on the screen in front of them (10%).

Parental monitoring and time regulation on children usage of gadgets are two important aspects to be considered. Table 4.13 shows time limits set by the parents.

Table 4.13: Time Limits Set on Electronic Gadgets by Parents (N=200)

Item	Number	Percentage
No time sets	50	25
30 min/day	35	17
1 hour/day	63	32
2 hours/day	38	19
3-4 hours/day	14	7

Findings from the above table indicate that one fourth (25%) of the parents do not regulate timings of children spending time with electronic gadgets. Whereas 32% of parents regulate the time for 1 hour per day, 19% of parents set 2 hours per day, 17% mothers restrict for half an hour and 7% set time for 3 to 4 hours per day.

The findings also reveal that 56% of children show temper tantrums when parents regulate timings and 44% of children willingly switch off the devices.

The data shows that one fourth (25%) of parents are not regulating their children screen time and 7% are allowing them to use gadgets for more than 3 hours on a typical working day. New recommendations in the American Association of Pediatrics Media and Young Minds Brief (2016) suggest that one hour of technology use is appropriate per day, inclusive of time spent at home and in early learning settings and across devices.

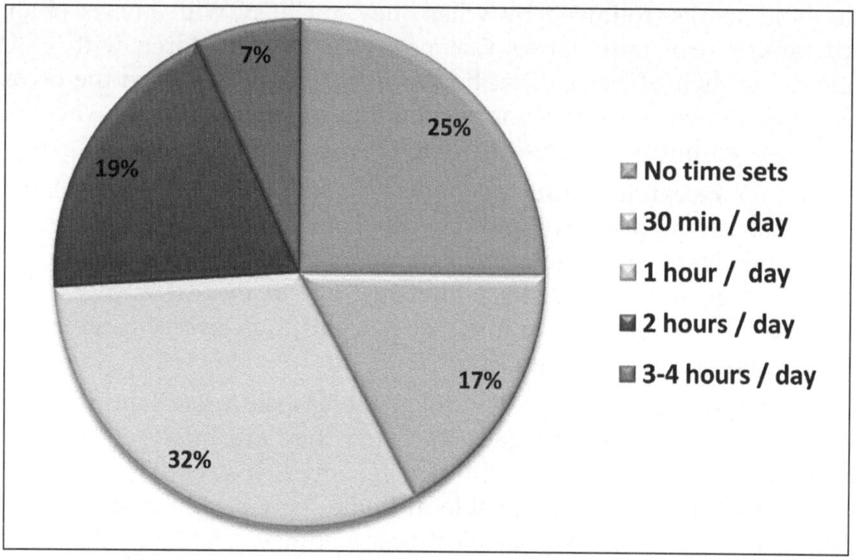

Fig. 4.5: Time Limits Set on Electronic Gadgets by Parents (N=200)

In the present study, the data revealed that around three fourth (73.5%) of families are nuclear and nearly one fourth (26.5%) are extended families. When children stay in the extended families, they can be engaged with more family members. Now a days most of the families being nuclear, it happens that when parents are busy with their regular and important tasks, they engage children with gadgets.

The specific occasions when parents allow children to use gadgets at home are presented in table 4.14.

Table 4.14: Occasions When Parents Allow Children to Use Electronic Gadgets (N=200)

Occasion	Total Score	Rank Order
To make him/her complete meal faster	446	1
When busy with household activities	408	2
When busy with guests, to engage the child	299	3
While doing office work at home	288	4
While parent is watching favourite programmes in TV/computer etc.	285	5
When going out, to engage the child	277	6

The above data was arranged in rank order based on the obtained total raw scores. The findings reveal that majority of parents are allowing children to use gadgets during meal time and this occasion obtained first rank. Second rank shows that parents allow when they are busy with household works, followed by when they are busy with guests obtained third rank, fourth rank shows that parents engage children with gadgets while doing their office work at home. Fifth rank obtained on the occasion when parents watch their favorite programmes and sixth rank shows that when they go out, to engage their children parents provide gadgets.

Similar research conducted by McCloskey etal (2017) revealed that 38% of parents occasionally and 12% of them daily engage children with electronic gadgets while doing their household tasks. Forty percent of them allow children to use gadgets while they are in the car and 20% allow when they are in the restaurants. Six percent of parents engage children with gadgets during meal time.

Thus it is clearly evident that due to increased nuclear families, parents are engaging children with gadgets when they are busy with their day today activities. If they have different resources like books, games, toys, craft material, puzzles etc available at home, parents can engage children with such activities instead of electronic gadgets. The data on available resources at home is presented in the table seventeen.

Table 4.15: Resources Available at Home (N=200)

Resources	Total Score N (%)	Rank order
Toys	196 (98)	1
Books	155 (78)	2
Games & Sports	152 (76)	3
Puzzles & building blocks	151 (76)	4
Craft material	134 (67)	5

It is observed from the above data that almost all (98%) houses with preschoolers are equipped with toys. Seventy eight percent of families are having books, followed by games and sports (76%) material, indoor games like puzzles and building blocks (76%) and 67% of families have craft material available at home.

When parents engage children with the above mentioned resources, it would be helpful for children to develop their fine motor skills, vocabulary, concentration, cognitive skills and creativity.

Preschool is the stage we can incorporate book reading habit and parents play a major role in motivating the children. Children and mothers interests about reading books and their reading preferences are presented in table 4.16.

Table 4.16: Reading Habits of Children (N=200)

Children and Mothers' Interest about Reading Books			
Item	**Children's Interest N (%)**	**Mothers' Interest N (%)**	**X^2 test**
Not at all interested	19 (9.5)	13 (6.5)	4.94@
Shows little interest	32 (16.0)	20 (10.0)	
Somewhat interested	42 (21.0)	46 (23.0)	
Very much interested	107 (53.5)	121 (60.5)	
Children and Mothers' Reading Preferences			
Item	**Children's Preference N (%)**	**Mothers' Preference N (%)**	**X^2 test**
Reading books	55 (27.5)	73 (36.5)	8.94*
Reading in electronic gadgets	23 (11.5)	9 (4.5)	
Both	44 (22.0)	46 (23.0)	
None	78 (39.0)	72 (36.0)	

Sixty percent of mothers and 53% of children are very much interested in reading books. Six percent of mothers and nine percent of children are not at all interested in reading books. No significant association found between children's and mothers' interests in reading books. However significant association was found between children's and mothers' reading preferences. The obtained chi-square value is 8.94 which is higher than the table value at 0.05 level. Figure 4.6 shows time spent by children reading books.

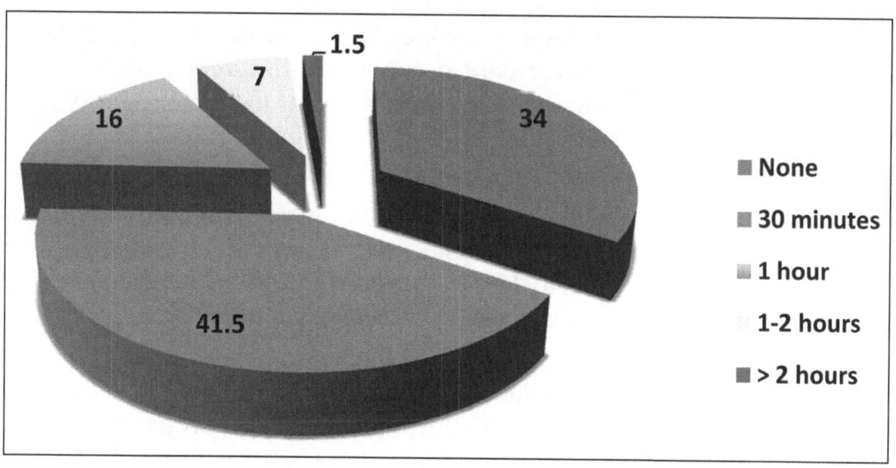

Fig. 4.6: Time Spent by Children in Reading Books

The findings reveals that one third (34%) of children are not spending time with books at all. Majority (41.5%) of preschool children are spending time with books like story books, comics, picture books for half-an-hour in a day, 16% of them are spending for one hour and 7% of children are reading books for more than one hour in a day with the help of their parents.

Research revealed that parents play a major role in incorporating reading habits among children. A study demonstrates that parental influence is a key factor on children's motivation to read as well as the development of life-long reading habits (Edmunds and Bauserman, 2006).

Koskinen *et.al.*, (2000) stated that access to reading material at home as well as parent-child interaction are often cited as two important factors in children's vocabulary and reading growth.

Another study showed that when children were asked about who gave them ideas for books to read for fun, parents were most often mentioned (77%), followed by teacher or librarian (57%), and friends (56%). However, parents were concerned about the effect electronic devices have on the time their children spend reading books for fun (Sinek and Sparkman, 2013).

The above studies demonstrate that parental influence is a key factor in motivating children to read books. When parents encourage children for book reading, children can develop vocabulary, language skills and thus their screen time will be reduced.

PERCEPTIONS OF MOTHERS TOWARDS CHILDREN'S USAGE OF ELECTRONIC GADGETS

Studies have shown both positive and negative impact on usage of electronic gadgets and children's development. Between the ages zero to six, rapid growth and development occur across different domains and it depends on numerous factors. Screen time is one of the major factors which influence children on their developmental domains.

Although findings of various studies revealed the increased screen time among young children, there is limited data available on parents' awareness and perceptions on children usage of electronic gadgets. In this study, an attempt is made to know the perceptions of mothers towards children usage of gadgets. The results are presented below.

Table 4.17 shows that majority (81.5%) of mothers agreed with the statement *"electronic gadgets influence children to develop language skills"*. They opined that when children watch different language progammes in the gadgets, they can pick up new vocabulary and learn new languages with ease. These results are in line with Hanna (2016) study which stated that parents perceptions were positively associated child technology use with language development.

Table 4.17: Perceptions of Mothers towards Children Usage of Electronic Gadgets (N=200)

S.No.	Statement	Agreed N (%)	Disagreed N (%)
	Electronic gadgets influence children to		
1.	develop language skills	163 (81.5%)	37 (18.5%)
2.	develop reading and writing skills	82 (41.0%)	118 (59.0%)
3.	reduce their outdoor play time	193 (97.0%)	7 (3.0%)
4.	develop social skills	116 (58.0%)	84 (42.0%)
5.	develop emotional skills	97 (48.5%)	103 (51.5%)
6.	develop cognitive skills	134 (67.0%)	66 (33.0%)
7.	develop gender stereotypic behaviour	159 (79.5%)	41 (20.5%)
8.	show aggressive and violent behaviour	162 (81.0%)	38 (19.0%)
9.	develop creativity	154 (77.0%)	46 (23.0%)
10.	develop moral values	94 (47.0%)	106 (53.0%)
11.	develop attention and concentration	109 (54.5%)	91 (45.5%)
12.	Children spending more time with electronic gadgets creates health problems	173 (86.5%)	27 (13.5%)
13.	Electronic gadgets create positive influence on children's academic performance	111 (55.5%)	89 (44.5%)
14.	Commercial ads influence children to seek kids' products	160 (80.0%)	40 (20.0%)
15.	Electronic gadgets create positive influence on children extra-curricular activities	80 (40.0%)	120 (60.0%)
16.	Usages of electronic gadgets induce healthy eating habits	61 (30.0%)	139 (70.0%)
17.	Usage of electronic gadgets disturbs children sleeping pattern	154 (77.0%)	46 (23.0%)
18.	Electronic gadgets play an important role in making children adapt to technological trends	162 (81.0%)	38 (19.0%)
19.	Computer based games diminish the time spent on indoor activities	173 (86.5%)	27 (13.5%)
20.	Electronic gadgets have lots of fun things to keep children entertained	172 (86.0%)	28 (14.0%)
21.	I am concerned that my child may become addicted to electronic gadgets in the future	143 (71.5%)	57 (28.5%)
22.	I worry about my child's exposure to media during my absence	141 (70.5%)	59 (29.5%)
23.	Electronic gadgets have lots of educational content that teaches important lessons	155 (78.0%)	45 (22.0%)
24.	Family's viewing of screen time has taken over the family time	158 (79.0%)	42 (21.0%)

The findings reveal that 59% of mothers disagreed to the statement *"electronic gadgets influence children to develop reading and writing skills"*. Children need to develop fine motor skills for writing readiness but when they spend time with gadgets, they will not get opportunity to develop required skills. Judge etal (2006) found that children's frequent use of computer programs for reading was negatively correlated with their reading achievement.

Almost all (97%) the mothers agreed up on the statement *"children's time with electronic gadgets reduces their outdoor play time"*. It is known that the current generation children are spending more time with gadgets than outdoor play. Gachuru (2012) reported that majority (60%) of children in his study preferred to watch TV rather than play with friends and around 40% of children preferred playing with friends.

Fifty eight percent mothers accepted the statement *"electronic gadgets influence children to develop social skills"*. Co-viewing and parental interactions would be helpful for social development of children. Similar results were found in the Erikson's institute report (2016), 42% of parents mentioned that technology benefited their children's social interaction skills.

Nearly half of the mothers (48.5%) agreed and other 51.5% disagreed to the statement *"electronic gadgets influence children to develop emotional skills"*. Children learn and exhibit emotions from the environment. Family, neighbourhood and school will help them to acquire different emotions and self-regulation. Gani (2016) found the negative effect invoked by gadget on child's socio-emotional skills. He stated that the habit of playing gadget will result in dependency behavior which can destruct child's social and emotional development. It will cause lack of socialization in the community and this will be continued from childhood to adulthood.

Majority (67%) of the mothers opined that *"electronic gadgets influence children to develop cognitive skills"*. Mothers expressed that interactive and activity based apps like puzzles, joining the dots, matching, guessing games etc are helpful for their children to develop cognitive skills.

Fish *et.al* (2008) found children computer access at home positively correlated with their cognitive development.

A greater percentage of mothers (79.5%) have agreed with the statement *"electronic gadgets influence children to develop gender stereotypic behaviour"*. Technology plays an important role to develop stereotypic traits among children. Generally, boys prefer to play with mechanical toys and girls play with dolls. Their preference in the viewing programs also varies. Few mothers shared that girls are fascinated with cartoon characters like Dora, Barbie, Chutki, Anna, Elsa etc whereas boys like Power rangers, Pokemon, Ben10 etc.

Eighty one percent of mothers accepted that *"electronic gadgets influence children to show aggressive and violent behaviour"*. Children perceive cartoon characters as role models and imitate them. Mothers expressed that especially boys prefer watching violent cartoon programs and they tend to imitate the characters. Numerous studies are indicated that violent content may lead to aggressive and impulsive behaviour among children. Conners-Burrow *et.al* (2011) reported in their study that children's viewing of age-inappropriate content of television programs was related to their aggressive and hyperactive behavior problems.

Seventy seven percent of mothers agreed with the statement that *"electronic gadgets influence children to develop creativity"*. Developing aesthetic sense through gadgets depends on the type of programs children watch and creative apps like colouring etc will help them to enhance creative skills.

Fifty three percent of mothers disagreed with the statement *"electronic gadgets influence children to develop moral values"*. Children will develop moral and ethical values when adults teach them what is correct and what is wrong. It can be inculcated through mythological stories, positive reinforcement etc. Unless properly explained, preschool children may not be able to develop moral values through gadgets.

More than half (54.5%) of the mothers agreed and nearly half (45.5%) of them have disagreed that *"electronic gadgets influence children to develop attention and concentration"*. However earlier research indicated negative association between children television viewing and their attention. A longitudinal study found positive correlation between early television exposure and subsequent symptoms of attention problems at age seven (Christaskiks *et.al*, 2004).

Majority (86.5%) of mothers perceived that *"children spending more time with electronic gadgets creates health problems in them such as obesity, visual problems etc"*. Generally when children are watching television or using any gadget, they do not concentrate on their body posture which may lead to health issues. Several research findings revealed the gadget usage of children and its impact on their health problems. Dietz and Gortmaker (1985) reported that each additional hour of TV viewing per week increased the risk of obesity by two percent. In another study, Stettler *et.al.* (2001) showed significant association between electronic game use and obesity, with nearly a 2-fold increased risk of obesity for every hour spent playing electronic games daily.

More than half (55.5%) of mothers agreed and 45.5% mothers disagreed with the statement *"electronic gadgets create positive influence on children's academic performance"*. Children's improvement in academic performance through gadgets depends upon the content they watch. When children watch educational programs, it will enhance their knowledge. According to Erikson's institute's report (2016), 56% of parents believed that their child's technology use promotes school readiness and 54% associate technology use with having an impact on success in school.

Eighty percent of mothers opined that *"commercial ads influence children to seek kids' products"*. Mothers mentioned that often their children are influenced by the attractive ads and branded products. They also reported that sometimes children throw tantrums to get the products which shown in the television programs and advertisements. Sixty six percent of parents mentioned in a study that "commercial ads and messages aimed to attract young children" (Erikson's institute report, 2016).

For the statement of *"electronic gadgets create positive influence on children extra-curricular activities"*, majority (60%) of mothers have disagreed. They mentioned that spending time for extra-curricular activities like swimming, dance, karate, music etc is more fruitful for children than screen time.

Seventy percent of the mothers disagreed to the statement *"usages of electronic gadgets induce healthy eating habits"*. Mostly we can see children having food sitting in front of the television or while using a gadget. They do not give attention to what they are eating and how much they are consuming. These kind of practices may lead to unhealthy food habits. Studies have shown the negative impact of screen time on food habits of children. A study revealed that TV viewing is inversely associated with intake of fruits and vegetables, which receive little air time despite their potential to promote health in various ways and protect against weight gain (Boynton, 2003).

Majority (77%) of mothers perceived that *"usage of electronic gadgets disturbs children sleeping pattern"*. Mothers expressed that due to bed time usage, children's sleep pattern is getting disturbed. Owens *et.al.* (1999) surveyed parents of 495 children from kindergarten through fourth grade on their children's television viewing and sleep habits. Results revealed that one fourth (25%) of children had a television in their bedroom. Television viewing habits were associated most significantly with sleep disturbances. Sleep disturbances were associated with increased daily television viewing and increased television viewing at bedtime, especially in the context of having a television set in the bedroom.

Eighty one percent of mothers agreed the statement *"electronic gadgets play an important role in making children adapt to technological trends"*. Strouse *et.al* (2014) reported that active parental engagement in technology use was shown to enhance children's learning.

Nearly eighty seven percentage (86.5%) of mothers accepted that *"computer based games diminish the time spent on indoor activities like board games, puzzles, reading books etc"*. Such indoor activities will help children to develop fine motor skills, eye-hand coordination, reading and writing readiness. But due to increased screen time, time spent on indoor games has been reduced. A study conducted by Wartella etal (2013) found that parents were more likely to use toys, books or television than a digital device to keep a child occupied. Likewise when a child was upset the parent was more likely to use a toy or activity to calm the child, with 17% of parents with mobile devices saying that it was 'somewhat likely' that they would do it to calm the child.

Eighty six percent of mothers agreed with the statement *"electronic gadgets have lots of fun things to keep children entertained"*. As gadgets have fun filled and entertaining content, children are easily getting attracted. Some parents reported that when they are busy with household tasks, they are engaging children with gadgets. In one study, many parents believed that media, particularly computers and television are important educational tools for engaging and entertaining children (Rideout and Hamel, 2006).

Around three fourth (71.5%) of the mothers have expressed that *"I am concerned that my child may become addicted to electronic gadgets in the future"*. As children are avid users of technology, mothers have expressed concerns that their children may get addicted to gadgets in the future. Monika Sharma (2012) reported in her study that "although advance technologies are quite essential in this fast moving era but addiction to such gadgets can cause health hazards as well as social imbalances".

Nearly seventy one percent (70.5%) of mothers also expressed concern about *"child's exposure to media when children are with someone else at home without parents"*. Mothers are worried for two major concerns during their absences – increased usage and content monitoring. These two are important aspects in controlling children. According to Ofcom report (2017), parents are worried about television content and the amount of time child spends watching TV. The report also mentioned that parents' concerns have been increased since 2016.

Seventy eight percent of mothers perceived that *"electronic gadgets have lots of educational content that teaches important lessons"*. Educational programs and videos will make children to understand the concepts with ease and interest. In a similar study, parents perceived computers are favourable for children's learning. However, no relationship was found between the frequency with which children played computer games and the likelihood that they could read, but increased non-game computer use was associated with increased likelihood of reading (Calvert *et.al,* 2005).

Majority (79%) of mothers agreed with the statement *"family's viewing of screen time has taken over the family time"*. Mothers have expressed that gadgets have occupied their family time like meal time, bed time, outings etc. Interestingly they have also shared that they feel incomplete without gadgets. Ling and Yttri (2006) reported that "cell phones and other new handheld devices have undermined family practices such as mealtimes and have established new generational boundaries.

Thus it is evident that with the increased use of technology among families, most of the mothers have positive perceptions towards children usage of electronic gadgets. Turow (1999) reported in his study that majority (70%) of parents in households with computers said that children can discover fascinating and useful things on the internet and 60% said that children without access to the internet were at a disadvantage compared to their peer who had internet access.

Age and Mothers' Perceptions towards Children Usage of Electronic Gadgets

Mothers play major role in shaping children at young age. Maternal age, education and occupation create an impact on parenting. Mean perception scores of below and above 30 years age group mothers towards children's usage of electronic gadgets is presented in the table 4.18.

Table 4.18: Mean Scores of Below and Above 30 Years Age Group Mothers on their Perceptions towards Children Usage of Electronic Gadgets (N=200)

S.No.	Statement	<30 years (N=76)		>30 years (N=124)		't' Value
	Electronic gadgets influence children to	Mean	SD	Mean	SD	
1.	develop language skills	2.87	0.38	2.71	0.58	2.34*
2.	develop reading and writing skills	2.45	0.60	2.24	0.64	2.29*
3.	reduce their outdoor play time	2.04	0.20	2.04	0.24	0.03@
4.	develop social skills	2.68	0.52	2.40	0.66	3.33*
5.	develop emotional skills	2.50	0.60	2.34	0.66	1.77@
6.	develop cognitive skills	2.79	0.57	2.57	0.70	2.38*
7.	develop gender stereotypic behaviour	1.97	0.52	2.11	0.77	1.53@
8.	show aggressive and violent behaviour	2.12	0.65	2.03	0.61	0.93@
9.	develop creativity	2.84	0.54	2.77	0.65	0.89@
10.	develop moral values	2.63	0.68	2.33	0.71	2.93*
11.	develop attention and concentration	2.71	0.65	2.41	0.73	3.01*
12.	Children spending more time with electronic gadgets creates health problems	2.00	0.61	2.22	0.68	2.37*
13.	Electronic gadgets create positive influence on children's academic performance	2.63	0.59	2.48	0.70	1.60@

(Table Contd...)

14.	Commercial ads influence children to seek kids' products	2.04	0.77	2.02	0.66	0.23@
15.	Electronic gadgets create positive influence on children extra-curricular activities	2.37	0.59	2.21	0.75	1.67@
16.	Usages of electronic gadgets induce healthy eating habits	2.18	0.56	2.24	0.70	0.64@
17.	Usage of electronic gadgets disturbs children sleeping pattern	2.91	0.57	2.90	0.68	0.14@
18.	Electronic gadgets play an important role in making children adapt to technological trends	2.88	0.52	2.88	0.55	0.03@
19.	Computer based games diminish the time spent on indoor activities	1.96	0.66	2.18	0.64	2.30*
20.	Electronic gadgets have lots of fun things to keep children entertained	2.95	0.56	2.98	0.52	0.36@
21.	I am concerned that my child may become addicted to electronic gadgets in the future	2.03	0.65	2.29	0.74	2.64*
22.	Child's exposure to media when children are with someone else at home without parents	2.11	0.62	2.29	0.67	1.98*
23.	Electronic gadgets have lots of educational content that teaches important lessons	2.87	0.62	2.81	0.50	0.64@
24.	Family's viewing of screen time has taken over the family time	1.97	0.63	2.11	0.75	1.41@

* Significant at 0.05 level
@ Not Significant

It can be observed from the above table that out of 24 items, the two groups differed significantly on 10 statements. Of these ten items, mothers of below 30 years scored higher on 6 items compared to the mothers of above 30 years. Mothers of above 30 years scored higher on the remaining 4 items than the mothers of below 30 years age group. The below figure demonstrates the mean scores of age and perceptions of mothers towards children usage of electronic gadgets.

The results reveal that mothers of younger age group perceived positive influence of electronic gadgets more than the mothers of above 30 years age group. Below 30 years age group mothers opined that electronic gadgets influence children to develop *language, reading and writing, social, cognitive skills and moral values. They also felt that gadgets are useful for developing children's attention and concentration.*

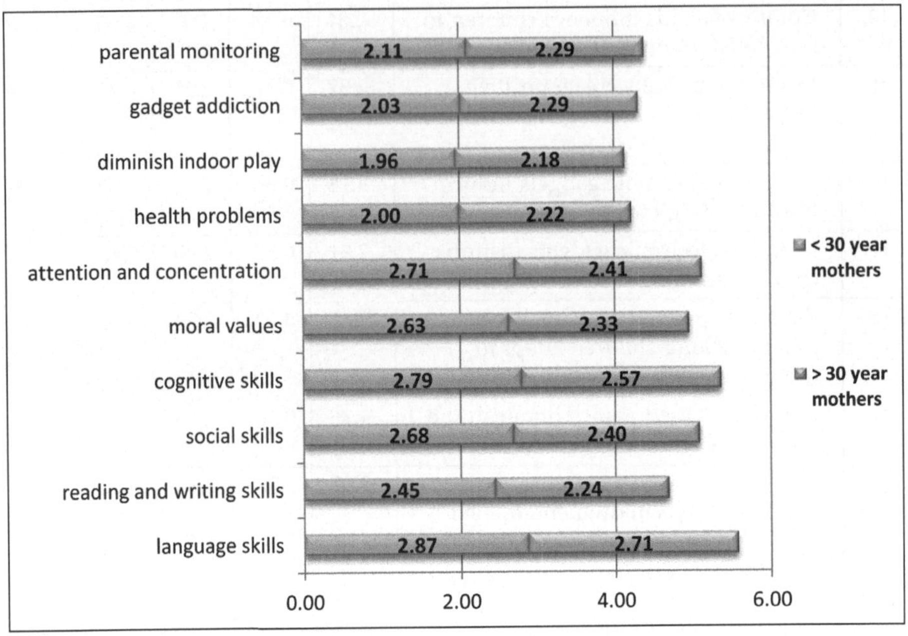

Fig. 4.7: Mean Scores of Below and above 30 Year Age Group Mothers on their Perceptions towards Children Usage of Electronic Gadgets

Whereas, mothers of above 30 year age group perceived negative effects of electronic gadgets more than the below 30 years age group. They believed that gadget usage causes *health problems* and diminish the time spent on *indoor activities* like board games, puzzles, books etc. Elder age group also expressed concerns like *gadget addiction* and their children *exposure to media during their absence.*

The Null Hypothesis Stated: *"Mothers' age has no effect on their perceptions towards children usage of electronic gadgets"*. The results demonstrated that mothers of preschool children differ significantly on 10 out of 24 statements of perceptions towards children usage of electronic gadgets. Hence the null hypothesis could be rejected. Younger group mothers have positive perceptions towards gadget usage whereas above 30 years age group mothers are more concerned about children health issues and gadget addiction.

Education and Mothers' Perceptions towards Children Usage of Electronic Gadgets

Mother's education is another important aspect which influences child rearing practices. Education provides knowledge and understanding for better parenting styles. Magnauson etal (2009) reported in his study that "increases in mother's education are linked to young children's expressive and receptive language skills".

Mean scores of Undergraduate and Postgraduate mothers on their perceptions towards children usage of electronic gadgets are presented in the table 4.19.

Table 4.19: Mean Scores of Undergraduate and Post Graduate Mothers on their Perceptions towards Children Usage of Electronic Gadgets (N=200)

S.No.	Statement	UG (N=99)		PG (N=101)		't' Value
	Electronic gadgets influence children to	Mean	SD	Mean	SD	
1.	develop language skills	2.80	0.45	2.74	0.58	0.76@
2.	develop reading and writing skills	2.50	0.60	2.24	0.65	2.95*
3.	reduce their outdoor play time	2.04	0.20	2.04	0.24	0.03@
4.	develop social skills	2.56	0.56	2.47	0.69	1.02@
5.	develop emotional skills	2.45	0.63	2.35	0.65	1.19@
6.	develop cognitive skills	2.68	0.68	2.63	0.64	0.46@
7.	develop gender stereotypic behaviour	2.05	0.61	2.07	0.75	0.19@
8.	show aggressive and violent behaviour	2.13	0.60	2.00	0.65	1.49@
9.	develop creativity	2.85	0.54	2.74	0.67	1.22@
10.	develop moral values	2.51	0.75	2.31	0.64	2.01*
11.	develop attention and concentration	2.65	0.67	2.45	0.75	2.03*
12.	Children spending more time with electronic gadgets creates health problems	1.89	0.57	1.89	0.73	0.02@
13.	Electronic gadgets create positive influence on children's academic performance	2.60	0.62	2.49	0.70	1.18@
14.	Commercial ads influence children to seek kids' products	2.06	0.70	1.99	0.71	0.71@
15.	Electronic gadgets create positive influence on children extra-curricular activities	2.31	0.66	2.23	0.72	0.87@
16.	Usages of electronic gadgets induce healthy eating habits	2.12	0.65	2.32	0.64	2.19*
17.	Usage of electronic gadgets disturbs children sleeping pattern	2.81	0.65	2.99	0.62	2.02*
18.	Electronic gadgets play an important role in making children adapt to technological trends	2.85	0.50	2.91	0.57	0.82@
19.	Computer based games diminish the time spent on indoor activities	1.92	0.60	1.82	0.70	1.06@
20.	Electronic gadgets have lots of fun things to keep children entertained	2.93	0.43	3.00	0.62	0.94@

(Table Contd…)

21.	I am concerned that my child may become addicted to electronic gadgets in the future	2.11	0.64	2.18	0.78	0.67@
22.	Child's exposure to media when children are with someone else at home without parents	2.22	0.58	2.21	0.73	0.15@
23.	Electronic gadgets have lots of educational content that teaches important lessons	2.84	0.51	2.83	0.58	0.09@
24.	Family's viewing of screen time has taken over the family time	2.11	0.57	2.01	0.82	1.02@

* Significant at 0.05 level

@ Not Significant

The above table shows that out of 24 items, the two groups differed significantly on 5 statements. Among these five items, UG mothers scored higher on 3 items and PG mothers scored higher in the remaining 2 items.

It is evident from the findings that undergraduate mothers have more positive perceptions towards children usage of electronic gadgets as compared to post graduate mothers. Undergraduate mothers perceived that usage of electronic gadgets is helpful for children to develop *reading* and *writing skills, moral values, attention and concentration*. While post graduate mothers perceived more on negative effects of gadget usage than undergraduate mothers. They opined that gadget usage leads to unhealthy *eating habits* and disturbance in *sleeping pattern*. Figure 4.8 portrays the mean scores of UG and PG mothers on their perceptions towards children usage of electronic gadgets.

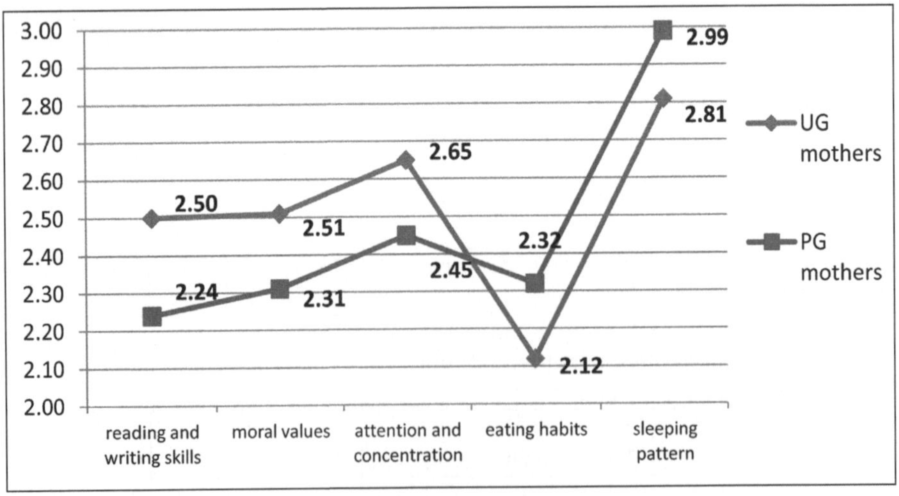

Fig. 4.8: Mean Scores of UG and PG Mothers on their Perceptions towards Children Usage of Electronic Gadgets

The Null Hypothesis Stated: *"Mothers' education has no effect on their perceptions towards children usage of electronic gadgets"*. In the present study, undergraduate and post graduate mothers differed significantly on five statements out of twenty four. Undergraduate mothers have more positive perceptions regarding gadget usage than post graduate mothers. Whereas post graduate mothers are more worried about child's eating and sleeping disturbances caused by electronic gadgets than undergraduate mothers. Thus the null hypothesis could be rejected.

In a study, Nikken and Schols (2015) reported that mothers more often apply supervision than fathers, and lower educated parents more often use technical restrictions on the child's media use than higher-educated parents.

Working and Non-working Mothers' Perceptions towards Children Usage of Electronic Gadgets

Mother's occupation is an important factor to be considered. Pasqua and Mancini (2012) have studied on working and non-working mothers' actual time spending with their children. Results shown that working mothers, with respect to non-working ones, tend to reduce the "basic care" time, but not "quality time" devoted for their children. Mother's occupation influences their thinking and perceptions. Mean scores of working and non-working mothers on their perceptions towards children's usage of electronic gadgets are presented in figure 4.9 and table 4.20.

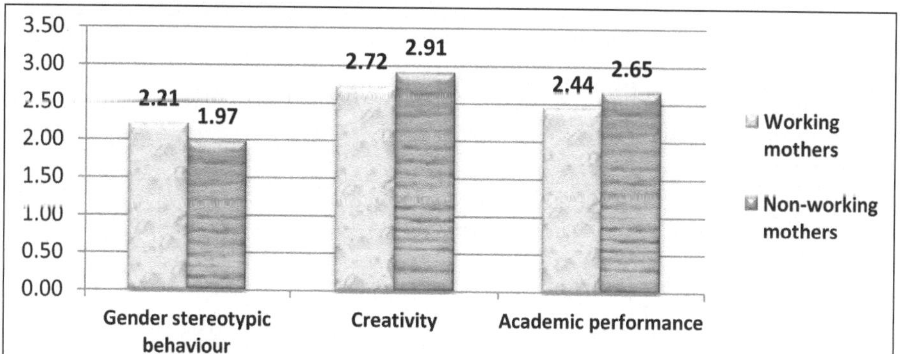

Fig. 4.9: Mean Scores of Working and Non-working mothers on their Perceptions towards Children Usage of Electronic Gadgets

The results reveal that out of 24 items, perceptions of working and non-working mothers did not differ significantly on 21 items. Whereas, working mothers have more positive perceptions that usage of gadgets is helpful for children's *creativity* and *academic performance* than non-working mothers. The differences are significant at 0.05 level. In contrast, non-working mothers are significantly more concerned that usage of gadgets create *gender stereotypic behaviour* among preschool children than working mothers.

Table 4.20: Mean Scores of Working and Non-working Mothers on their Perceptions towards Children Usage of Electronic Gadgets (N=200)

S.No.	Statement	Working (N=104)		Non-working (N=96)		't' value
	Electronic gadgets influence children to	Mean	SD	Mean	SD	
1.	develop language skills	2.73	0.58	2.81	0.44	1.13@
2.	develop reading and writing skills	2.31	0.61	2.33	0.66	0.28@
3.	reduce their outdoor play time	2.06	0.27	2.02	0.14	1.21@
4.	develop social skills	2.44	0.67	2.58	0.57	1.61@
5.	develop emotional skills	2.38	0.64	2.42	0.64	0.35@
6.	develop cognitive skills	2.63	0.70	2.68	0.62	0.45@
7.	develop gender stereotypic behaviour	2.21	0.77	1.97	0.57	2.53*
8.	show aggressive and violent behaviour	2.06	0.59	2.07	0.67	0.17@
9.	develop creativity	2.72	0.67	2.91	0.53	2.21*
10.	develop moral values	2.40	0.69	2.41	0.72	0.02@
11.	develop attention and concentration	2.46	0.74	2.59	0.69	1.31@
12.	Children spending more time with electronic gadgets creates health problems	1.87	0.67	1.92	0.64	0.55@
13.	Electronic gadgets create positive influence on children's academic performance	2.44	0.68	2.65	0.63	2.19*
14.	Commercial ads influence children to seek kids' products	2.07	0.71	1.98	0.70	0.88@
15.	Electronic gadgets create positive influence on children extra-curricular activities	2.23	0.74	2.31	0.64	0.84@
16.	Usages of electronic gadgets induce healthy eating habits	2.15	0.66	2.29	0.63	1.50@
17.	Usage of electronic gadgets disturbs children sleeping pattern	2.95	0.70	2.84	0.57	1.20@
18.	Electronic gadgets play an important role in making children adapt to technological trends	2.88	0.55	2.88	0.53	0.13@
19.	Computer based games diminish the time spent on indoor activities	1.83	0.70	1.92	0.59	0.98@
20.	Electronic gadgets have lots of fun things to keep children entertained	3.00	0.57	2.93	0.49	0.97@
21.	I am concerned that my child may become addicted to electronic gadgets in the future	2.11	0.74	2.19	0.69	0.81@

(Table Contd...)

22.	Child's exposure to media when children are with someone else at home without parents	2.22	0.62	2.21	0.69	0.14@
23.	Electronic gadgets have lots of educational content that teaches important lessons	2.84	0.58	2.83	0.52	0.04@
24.	Family's viewing of screen time has taken over the family time	2.07	0.73	2.05	0.69	0.15@

* Significant at 0.05 level

@ Not Significant

The Null Hypothesis Sated: *"Mothers' working status has no effect on their perceptions towards children usage of electronic gadgets"*. The results have shown that perceptions of working and non-working mothers differ significantly on 3 items. Working mothers have shown positive perceptions whereas non-working mothers are more concerned towards their children usage of electronic gadgets. Based on the results, the null hypothesis could be rejected.

It can be concluded from tables 4.18, 4.19 and 4.20 that mothers of below 30 years group, undergraduates and working have more positive perceptions towards gadgets usage of preschool children. Whereas, mothers belong to above 30 years age group, post graduates and non-working are more concerned about children health issues and gadget addiction.

Suggestions of Mothers towards Children Usage of Electronic Gadgets

As technology has become inseparatable part of modern life, children are exploring to different varieties of gadgets. If mothers are aware of preschool children recommended screen time, they can regulate their children electronic gadget usage time. Figure 4.10 portrays mothers' awareness on recommended screen time of preschool children.

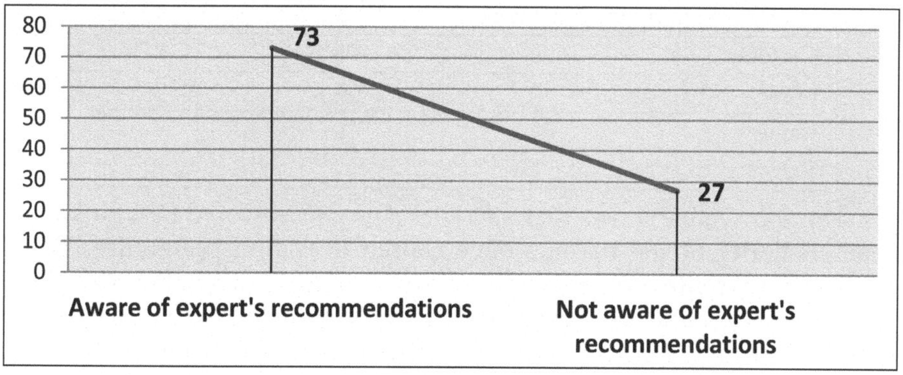

Fig. 4.10: Mothers' Knowledge on Recommended Screen Time for Preschool Children (N=200)

It can be observed from the figure shows that nearly three fourth (73%) of preschool mothers are aware of experts recommended screen time for their children. Whereas more than one fourth (27%) of the mothers do not have knowledge on experts recommendations.

The findings of previous section revealed that 25% of mothers do not regulate timings of children spending with electronic gadgets and 7% of mothers set for more than the recommended time i.e. above 4 hours per day. It is important for the mothers to know the suggestions and recommendations of experts like pediatricians and educationalists. According to their suggestions, limited screen time for preschool children is one hour per day. Parents co-view media with children will help them to understand what they are seeing and apply it to the world around them.

In a similar study, Adamiak (2015) investigated parent's knowledge about media use, recommendations for preschoolers and the amount of time individuals' report their children spend on electronic devices. Results showed that 78% of parents restricted their children's screen media viewing to less than 2 hours a day, the recommended amount. However, 22% of parents did not restrict their children's screen media viewing to less than two hours. Of these parents who did not restrict their children's viewing, 85% knew the recommendation is less than two hours.

Children's choice in viewing the programs and parents' preferences for their children to view programmes may differ. To understand mothers' preferred programmes for their children to watch, the data was analyzed in the rank order based on the obtained total raw scores. The least possible score is 200 and highest possible score is 600 and the finding presented in the below table.

Table 4.21: Programs Parents Prefer their Children to Watch (N=200)

Programme	Total Score	Rank Order
Educational programs/activities	468	1
Cartoons	438	2
Music	396	3
Games	370	4
Videos	354	5

The above table shows that *'educational programs'* scored first rank which means majority of the parents have chosen it as first preference. This is followed by parents' preference to *'cartoon channels'* which obtained second rank and next *'music'* acquired third rank. Fourth rank has been given to *'games'* and *'movie videos'* obtained fifth rank. Thus it is evident that majority of parents want their children to watch educational programs in the gadgets and they gave least preference to movie videos. Some parents expressed that they encourage their children to watch educational channels like National Geography, Discovery, Animal Planet etc. Few parents have also mentioned that co-viewing of such channels with their kids is great fun.

In a similar research, Rideout *et.al* (2003) reported that 96% of parents considered books are very important for their children intellectual development, 77% considered building blocks, 74% mentioned puzzles, 62% of parents preferred educational toys like talking books, 58% considered educational TV, 49% preferred educational videos, 43% mentioned educational computer games and 31% of the parents perceived educational websites are useful for their children development.

Erikson Institute Report (2016) suggested that parents need to strive for a healthy balance of technology engagement with their children and for parent-child experiences that require no technology at all. Use technology to support the joy of learning—to engage, empower, and inspire the child".

The quality of interaction between the mother and child is more important than the amount of time spent together. Quality time plays a critical role in maintaining the mother-child bond (Bowlby, 1980). Hence it is important to understand the amount of quality time parents spend with their children as it is an important factor for their development in the preschool stage.

The below figure shows how much quality time mothers are spending with their children on a working day. Quality time includes mothers' conversing with their children, bed time stories, reading books, home works, playing games, involve in craft activities etc.

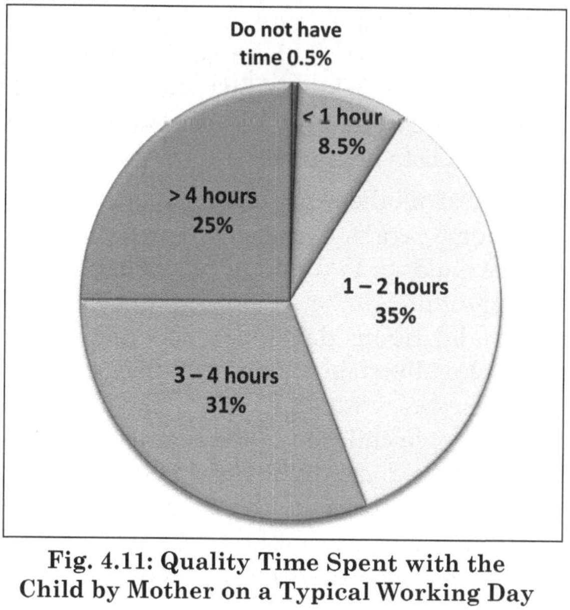

Fig. 4.11: Quality Time Spent with the Child by Mother on a Typical Working Day

The above findings reveal that 35% of mothers are spending 1-2 hours quality time with their children on a working day. Nearly one third (31%) of mothers are spending 3-4 hours, one fourth (25%) of mothers are spending more than 4 hours with their children in a day. Few mothers (8.5%) agreed that they are able to spend less than one hour with their children on a working day. One mother (0.5%) mentioned that she is not getting time to spend quality time with her child due to longer working hours and household tasks. This quality time reduces children's screen time and it will be helpful for their physical, cognitive, language and social developments. On a typical working day, how mothers are spending time with their children is illustrated in the below table.

Table 4.22: Activities Done by the Child and Mother on a Typical Working Day (N=200)

	Number	Percentage
Playing with child	145	73
Story telling	123	62
Helping in the studies	112	56
Taking them for outings	81	41
Conversation with children	64	32
Doing art and craft activities	41	21
Involve children in the household activities	34	17
Teaching new things	32	16
Unable to spend time with my child due to busy schedule	5	3

Nearly three fourth (73%) of mothers mentioned that they play with their children every day. Most of them said they enjoy playing indoor games like building blocks, puzzles etc. Sixty two percent of mothers shared that they tell stories to their children. Mothers said, preschool children are very much interested in listening to stories and they enjoy bed time stories.

Fifty six percent of mothers mentioned that they help their children in completing the home works every day. Forty one percent of mothers shared that they take children to different places like shops, super markets, parks etc. Around one third (32%) of mothers mentioned that they talk to their children every day about day today activities, school activities etc. Twenty one percent of mothers mentioned that they enjoy drawing, coloring activities and craft works with their kids. Seventeen percent of them expressed that they involve children in the household tasks and 16% stated that they teach new things to children. Three percent of mothers mentioned that they are unable to spend time with their children due to busy work schedule and household tasks. Table 4.23 shows mothers' views and suggestions on children usage of electronic gadgets.

Table 4.23: Mothers' Suggestions on Children Usage of Electronic Gadgets (N=200)

Effect of Usage of Electronic Gadgets on Children		
	Number	**Percentage**
Electronic gadgets have both advantages and disadvantages	124	62
Gadgets will cause health problem in children	111	56
Parents need to monitor and guide children	102	51
Children can learn new things	98	49
Parents need to set time limits	90	45
Future addiction is a concern	68	34
Gadgets are useful for children	62	31
Gadget usage may lead to violent behavior	41	21
Gadget usage reduces the time spent on outdoor play	28	14
Avoid using the gadgets for children	10	5
Reasons for increased usage of electronic gadgets by children		
Parents are busy	141	71
Availability and easy access of gadgets	130	65
Lot of attractive features and apps which attract children	127	64
Entertainment	84	42
Increased nuclear families	55	28
As parents are using, children are imitating them	51	26
Single child	35	18
Lack of play area	32	16
Apartment culture	19	10
It became a status for parents to keep different gadgets at home and giving for children	16	8
Suggestions to engage children during free time		
Join them in activity/hobby classes	140	70
Provide variety of indoor games	136	68
Engage children in outdoor play	122	61
Take them for different places like zoo, parks etc	108	54
Tell them stories	64	32
Engage children with books	62	31
Engage children with relatives, neighbours and friends	32	16
Encourage children to participate in the household activities	22	11
Prepare time schedule for whole day and implement	3	2

For the question *"effect of usage of electronic gadgets on children"*, sixty two percent of mothers stated that gadget usage has both advantages and disadvantages. Fifty six percent mentioned that gadgets will cause health problems like visual problems, obesity, sleeping disorders etc and 51% reported that parents need to monitor children usage of gadgets. Nearly half (49%) answered that children can learn new things. Forty five percent of mothers opined that parents need to set time limits and 34% of them expressed concern about future gadget addiction of their children. Thirty one percent opined that gadgets are very useful and in contrast, 21% reported that gadget usage may lead to violent behaviour among children. Fourteen percent of mothers expressed that gadget usage reduces play time and 5% said it is better to avoid using gadgets.

The next question is *"Reasons for increased usage of electronic gadgets by children"*. For this question, Around three fourth (71%) of mothers mentioned that due to increased dual earning families, parents are not able to spend enough time with their children and as a result children are spending more time with the gadgets. Sixty five percent of mothers answered that availability of various electronic gadgets for 24/7 and 64% of mothers reported that because gadgets have wide variety of features and apps children are getting attracted towards them. Forty two percent of mothers stated that gadgets entertain children. Twenty eight percent mentioned that due to increase in families, there is no one to engage children so they are spending time with electronic gadgets rather with family members. Nearly one fourth (26%) of mothers opined that as parents are avid users of gadgets, children are learning and imitating them. Eighteen percent answered that due to single child, the child does not have siblings to play and so spent time with gadgets. Sixteen percent of mothers said due to lack of play area and 10% stated that because of apartment culture children are using gadgets. Eight percent of mothers reported that now a days, it became a status symbol for parents to keep different gadgets at home and give to their children.

The last question is *"Suggestions to engage children during free time?"* For this question, majority (70%) of mothers mentioned that children should be joined in the hobby classes like dance, music, karate, swimming etc. Sixty eight percent of mothers stated that variety of indoor games can be provided and 61% said that children can be engaged with outdoor games. Fifty four percent answered that children should be taken to different places like zoo, parks, shopping etc.

Nearly one third (32%) opined that children can be engaged with stories and story books and teach them moral values. Similarly 31% expressed that need to engage children with book reading. Sixteen percent of them answered that children can be engaged with neighbours, relatives and friends so that it will be helpful for their social development. Eleven percent stated that children need to be engaged with simple household tasks and 2% suggested to prepare a time table with various activities and it should be implemented.

Hence it can be concluded from the above answers that most of the mothers are spending time with their children in playing, storytelling and assisting with school works. Mothers have mixed opinions about gadget usage. They expressed both positive and negative concerns towards their children usage of electronic gadgets. Majority of mothers opined that due to increased dual earning families and availability of gadgets, children usage time has been increased. They stated the best ways to engage children are hobby classes, indoor and outdoor games etc.

PERCEPTIONS OF TEACHERS TOWARDS CHILDREN'S USAGE OF ELECTRONIC GADGETS

After home, children spend considerable time in the school. Preschool teachers play vital role in the early educational settings in shaping child's behaviour. They develop bonding and communication with young children. As they influence children in many ways, it is essential to understand preschool teachers' perceptions towards children usage of electronic gadgets. In the present study, an attempt is made to understand the perceptions of teachers towards children usage of gadgets and the findings are presented in table 4.24.

The findings from table 4.24 reveal that majority (95%) of teachers agreed with the statement *"electronic gadgets influence children to develop language skills"*. They shared that young children are quick learners and they can easily pick up vocabulary from different programmes. Teachers also specified that by the time some children join in the preschool, some of them are already familiar with rhymes, alphabet, numbers etc which they are learning through gadgets. These results are in line with Ghavifekr (2015) study which stated that teachers' perceived technology has a positive effect on children's language awareness when it is used appropriately.

More than half (65%) of teachers perceived that *"electronic gadgets influence children to develop reading and writing skills"*. They mentioned that educational apps are helpful for children to develop these skills. When parents explore children to such educational apps, they can improve their reading and writing skills. However, indoor activities like clay molding, drawing, colouring etc are essential to develop fine motor skills. Bittman *et.al* (2011) found in his study that children's computer access at home is positively correlated with children's performance in reading.

Table 4.24: Perceptions of Teachers towards Children Usage of Electronic Gadgets (N=60)

S.No.	Statement Electronic gadgets influence children...	Agreed N (%)	Disagreed N (%)
1.	To develop language skills	57 (95%)	3 (5%)
2.	To develop reading and writing skills	39 (65%)	21 (35%)
3.	Reduces their outdoor play time	59 (98%)	1 (2%)
4.	To develop social skills	44 (73%)	16 (27%)
5.	To develop emotional skills	38 (63%)	22 (37%)
6.	To develop cognitive skills	48 (80%)	12 (20%)
7.	To develop gender stereotypic behaviour	54 (90%)	6 (10%)
8.	To show aggressive and violent behaviour	54 (90%)	6 (10%)
9.	To develop creativity	56 (93%)	4 (7%)
10.	To develop moral values	31 (52%)	29 (48%)
11.	To develop attention and concentration	32 (53%)	28 (47%)
12.	Children spending more time with electronic gadgets creates health problems	58 (97%)	2 (3%)
13.	Electronic gadgets create positive influence on children's academic performance	30 (50%)	30 (50%)
14.	Commercial ads influence children to seek kids' products	54 (90%)	6 (10%)
15.	Electronic gadgets create positive influence on children extra-curricular activities	31 (52%)	29 (48%)
16.	Usages of electronic gadgets induce healthy eating habits	13 (22%)	47 (78%)
17.	Usage of electronic gadgets disturbs children sleeping pattern	55 (92%)	5 (8%)
18.	Electronic gadgets play an important role in making children adapt to technological trends	54 (90%)	6 (10%)
19.	Computer based games diminish the time spent on indoor activities	55 (92%)	5 (8%)
20.	Electronic gadgets have lots of fun things to keep children entertained	56 (93%)	4 (7%)
21.	Electronic gadgets have lots of educational content that teaches important lessons	56 (93%)	4 (7%)
22.	Schools with digital class rooms improves quality of education	55 (92%)	5 (8%)

Almost all (98%) early childhood teachers accepted that *"children's time with electronic gadgets reduces their outdoor play time"*. They shared that outdoor play is an important activity for young children to develop gross-motor skills. But because of gadget usage, time spent on outdoor play has been reduced.

Nearly three fourth (73%) of teachers opined that *"electronic gadgets influence children to develop social skills"*. When children watch programs with parents and they converse while watching, peer group and family interactions during television time are helpful for their social development. Morrison and Krugman (2001) reported in their study that television viewing promotes "television talk" where family members and friends can establish a means for positive communication and social interaction. They also mentioned that television programmes can become "a topic of conversation" whilst giving "people something to talk about" and as a result, is contributing to social interaction between individuals.

Sixty three percent of teachers agreed upon the statement *"electronic gadgets influence children to develop emotional skills"*. They stated that preschool children observe different emotions in the cartoon programs and they would love to enact their favourate characters. Such activities will help children to develop emotional skills.

Majority (80%) of the teachers agreed with the statement that *"electronic gadgets influence children to develop cognitive skills"*. Studies have shown that maximum brain development happens below six years of age. Children can easily grasp the content through educational videos and gain knowledge. So gadgets are helpful for their better understanding and cognitive development.

Ninety percent of teachers accepted with the statement *"electronic gadgets influence children to develop gender stereotypic behaviour"*. Teachers shared that technology strongly influences children's thoughts and behavior. They develop gender stereotypic traits through cartoon programmes, videos, commercial ads etc.

Similarly 90% of teachers accepted that *"electronic gadgets influence children to show aggressive and violent behaviour"*. Teachers shared their observation that sometimes preschool children are playing violent games and hurting others by using different cartoon characters names. Especially it is happening during outdoor play time and generally boys tend to show such behaviour compared with girls. They mentioned that violent content leads to develop such aggressive and violent behavior among preschoolers. A comprehensive meta-analysis conducted by Anderson (2010) found that exposure to violent video games increases aggressive thoughts, angry feelings, physiologic arousal, hostile appraisals and aggressive behavior and decreases pro-social behavior and empathy among young children.

A greater percentage (93%) of preschool teachers agreed with the statement that *"electronic gadgets influence children to develop creativity"*. Teachers mentioned that creative development through gadgets can happen when children exposed to creative programs like MAD in Pogo channel, 5 minute crafts, DIY crafts etc. They suggested that parents can encourage children to watch such programs.

Fifty two percent of the teachers agreed and remaining half (48%) of them have disagreed that *"electronic gadgets influence children to develop moral values"*. Thus teachers have both positive and negative opinion on gadget usage and children moral development. Early childhood teachers opined that moral values can be taught through stories and books for better understanding.

In the same way around half (53%) of the teachers agreed and another half (47%) of them have disagreed that *"electronic gadgets influence children to develop attention and concentration"*. It shows that they have mixed view on children screen time and their attention and concentration. Some teachers mentioned that activities like problem solving puzzles, book reading, colouring etc are more useful for children to increase attention. Swing etal (2010) found that 'viewing television and playing video games are associated with increased subsequent attention problems in childhood, late adolescence and early adulthood.

Almost all (97%) teachers perceived that *"children spending more time with electronic gadgets creates health problems in them such as obesity, visual problems etc"*. Teaches reported that they are observing visual problems among children at very young age and the main cause is gadget usage. When children sit closely in front of the gadgets for longer hours, it will affect their vision. Parents need to constantly monitor children. They also shared that over weight among preschoolers is also increasing considerably. Stiglic and Viner (2019) found in their study that children with higher screen time tend to have a less healthy diet, a higher energy intake and more pronounced indicators of obesity.

Exactly half (50%) of teachers agreed and another half (50%) disagreed with the statement *"electronic gadgets create positive influence on children's academic performance"*. They expressed that it depends upon the programs children watch. When children watch educational content in the gadgets and if they can connect with real time situations, it will be helpful for their academic success.

Majority (90%) of the teachers perceived that *"commercial ads influence children to seek kids' products"*. Children can easily be influenced by commercial ads when compare with adults. As most of the ads target younger group, children will get attracted towards such products.

Nearly half (52%) of the teachers agreed and half (48%) disagreed with the statement of *"electronic gadgets create positive influence on children extra-curricular activities.* They shared that extra-curricular activities are helpful for children to develop several skills which are essential for their development. Parents need to divert children in learning such activities rather spending time with gadgets.

Seventy eight percent of the teachers disagreed to the statement *"usages of electronic gadgets induce healthy eating habits"*. Teachers reported that healthy eating habits and table manners should be inculcated in children during preschool stage. Both home and school take part in creating healthy eating habits among preschoolers.

For the statement *"usage of electronic gadgets disturbs children sleeping pattern"*, majority (92%) of teachers responded positively. They opined that bed time usage of gadgets creates such problems in children. They have also shared that sleeping disturbances can cause attention problems in the classroom activities which adversely affect their academic achievement. A study revealed that majority of teachers and parents were against children having technology in their bed rooms. Teachers were more vocally opposed on the grounds of impact on classroom behaviour and performance (Downey etal, 2007).

Ninety percent of preschool teachers agreed the statement *"electronic gadgets play an important role in making children adapt to technological trends"*. Researchers have paid attention to not only how technologies affect young children's learning across domains, but also how young children learn to use a variety of technologies, that is the development of digital literacy. In comparison with the traditional view of literacy, such new forms of literacy emphasize children's abilities to comprehend and create multimodal digital texts in order to communicate with texts or others (Bawden, 2008).

Most of the teachers (92%) accepted that *"computer based games diminish the time spent on indoor activities like board games, puzzles, reading books etc"*. They expressed that such indoor activities are helpful for children to develop pre-reading, pre-writing and pre-mathematical skills. These school readiness activities will help them for academic success. Wolf and Flewitt (2010) reported in their study that most of the teachers were concerned that children's frequent use of technology may impede their development.

Ninety three percent of teachers agreed with the statement *"electronic gadgets have lots of fun things to keep children entertained"*. With increased evolution in technology, new model gadgets with advance features and attractive programs are available for children. 3D animated programs are more attractive for young children. So teachers perceived that gadgets are engaging and entertaining children.

Majority (93%) of the teachers perceived that *"electronic gadgets have lots of educational content that teaches important lessons"*. Vandewater and Bickham (2004) found in their study that children's use of educational television with a cognitive curriculum was related to better reading scores and academic performance.

Significant (92%) number of teachers agreed with the statement "*schools with digital class rooms improves quality of education*". Preschool teachers expressed that augmented learning and virtual reality are very effective techniques in the modern era. Children learn subjects with interest and ease. Similar results found in a research conducted by Lindita and Fauzi (2017) stated that teachers agreed with the effectiveness of technology in the education. They agreed that technology increases student's academic achievement and enhances lifelong learning which is one of most important aims of learning in general.

Age and Teachers Perceptions towards Children Usage of Electronic Gadgets

With regard to teachers' variables, age is an important predictor which influences their beliefs and perceptions. Mean perception scores of below and above 30 year age group teachers towards children's usage of electronic gadgets presented in table 4.25.

Table 4.25: Mean Scores of below and above 30 Year Age Group Teachers on their Perceptions towards Children Usage of Electronic Gadgets (N=60)

S.No.	Statement	<30 years (N=29)		>30 years (N=31)		't' value
	Electronic gadgets influence children	Mean	SD	Mean	SD	
1.	To develop language skills	3.00	0.53	3.10	0.54	0.70@
2.	To develop reading and writing skills	2.55	0.57	2.48	0.63	0.44@
3.	Reduces their outdoor play time	1.55	0.51	1.45	0.57	0.72@
4.	To develop social skills	2.59	0.63	2.45	0.81	0.72@
5.	To develop emotional skills	2.66	0.55	2.65	0.66	0.06@
6.	To develop cognitive skills	2.79	0.41	2.68	0.79	0.72@
7.	To develop gender stereotypic behaviour	2.07	0.70	2.10	0.54	0.17@
8.	To show aggressive and violent behaviour	2.07	0.70	2.03	0.71	0.20@
9.	To develop creativity	3.20	0.58	2.85	0.60	2.30*
10.	To develop moral values	2.24	0.74	2.61	0.72	1.98*
11.	To develop attention and concentration	2.41	0.73	2.80	0.78	1.97*
12.	Children spending more time with electronic gadgets creates health problems	1.48	0.57	1.55	0.57	0.44@
13.	Electronic gadgets create positive influence on children's academic performance	2.34	0.72	2.48	0.68	0.77@
14.	Commercial ads influence children to seek kids' products	1.90	0.49	1.94	0.73	0.24@
15.	Electronic gadgets create positive influence on children extra-curricular activities	2.66	0.77	2.65	0.61	0.06@

(Table Contd...)

16.	Usages of electronic gadgets induce healthy eating habits	2.17	0.60	2.29	0.74	0.68@
17.	Usage of electronic gadgets disturbs children sleeping pattern	2.86	0.74	3.20	0.56	1.98*
18.	Electronic gadgets play an important role in making children adapt to technological trends	2.86	0.58	2.94	0.44	0.54@
19.	Computer based games diminish the time spent on indoor activities	1.76	0.79	1.84	0.64	0.43@
20.	Electronic gadgets have lots of fun things to keep children entertained	3.07	0.46	3.06	0.44	0.04@
21.	Electronic gadgets have lots of educational content that teaches important lessons	3.10	0.46	2.87	0.43	2.00*
22.	Schools with digital class rooms improves quality of education	3.41	0.47	3.06	0.63	2.42*

The above table reveals that out of 24 items, teachers of below 30 years and above 30 years differed significantly on 6 statements. Among these six items, teachers of below 30 years scored higher on 3 items and teachers of above 30 years scored higher on the remaining 3 items. Figure 4.12 illustrates the mean scores of below 30 years and above 30 years teachers on their perceptions towards children usage of electronic gadgets.

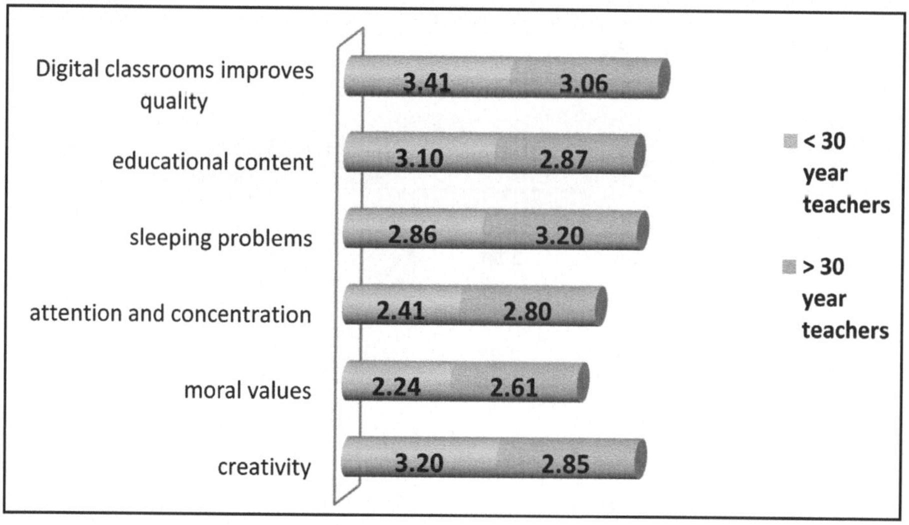

Fig. 4.12: Mean Scores of below above 30 years Teachers on their Perceptions towards Children Usage of Electronic Gadgets

It is evident that teachers of below 30 year age group have shown more positive perceptions on children usage of electronic gadgets compared with above 30 year age group. Below 30 year old age teachers opined that gadgets are useful for children *creative development* and gadgets have lot of *educational content* that teaches important lessons to children. They have also perceived that schools with *digital classrooms* improve quality of education.

Teachers of above 30 years believed that usage of electronic gadgets is helpful for children to develop *moral values, attention and concentration.* They have raised concern about children *sleeping disturbances* because of screen time.

The Null Hypothesis Stated: *"Teachers' age has no effect on their perceptions towards children usage of electronic gadgets"*. Based on the results of the present study, the null hypothesis could be rejected. Teachers of below 30 years and above 30 years age groups differed significantly on 6 statements. Comparatively, younger age group teachers have positive perceptions than elder age group teachers. Whereas above 30 year teachers expressed concern about gadget usage and sleeping disorders.

Education and Teachers Perceptions towards Children Usage of Electronic Gadgets

Teacher's education has an obvious influence on their perceptions. Mean scores of Undergraduate and Postgraduate teachers on their perceptions towards children usage of electronic gadgets is presented in figure 4.13 and table 4.26.

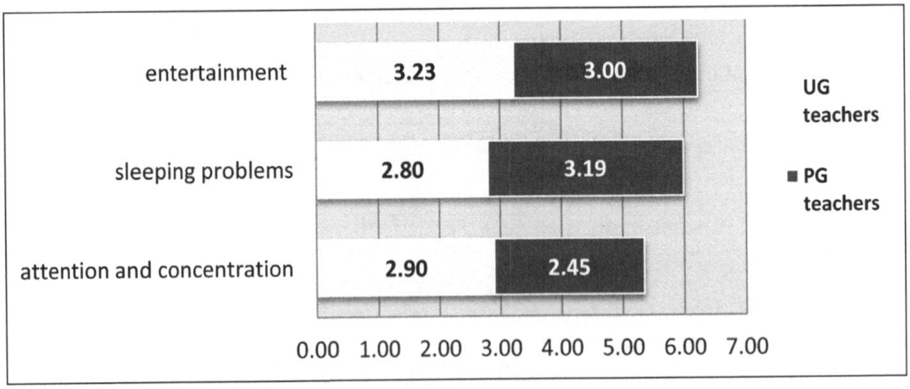

Fig. 4.13: Mean Scores of UG and PG Teachers on their Perceptions towards Children Usage of Electronic Gadgets

Table 4.26: Mean Scores of Undergraduate and Postgraduate teachers on their Perceptions towards Children Usage of Electronic Gadgets (N=60)

S.No.	Statement	UG (N=31)		PG (N=29)		't' Value
	Electronic gadgets influence children	Mean	SD	Mean	SD	
1.	To develop language skills	3.06	0.51	3.03	0.57	0.21@
2.	To develop reading and writing skills	2.42	0.62	2.62	0.56	1.31@
3.	Reduces their outdoor play time	1.48	0.57	1.52	0.51	0.24@
4.	To develop social skills	2.48	0.72	2.55	0.74	0.36@
5.	To develop emotional skills	2.55	0.62	2.76	0.58	1.36@
6.	To develop cognitive skills	2.68	0.75	2.79	0.49	0.71@
7.	To develop gender stereotypic behaviour	1.97	0.60	2.21	0.62	1.51@
8.	To show aggressive and violent behaviour	2.00	0.73	2.10	0.67	0.57@
9.	To develop creativity	3.06	0.51	2.97	0.68	0.63@
10.	To develop moral values	2.45	0.62	2.41	0.87	0.19@
11.	To develop attention and concentration	2.90	0.79	2.45	0.74	2.29*
12.	Children spending more time with electronic gadgets creates health problems	1.48	0.57	1.55	0.57	0.46@
13.	Electronic gadgets create positive influence on children's academic performance	2.39	0.76	2.45	0.63	0.34@
14.	Commercial ads influence children to seek kids' products	2.00	0.73	1.83	0.47	1.10@
15.	Electronic gadgets create positive influence on children extra-curricular activities	2.71	0.78	2.59	0.57	0.70@
16.	Usages of electronic gadgets induce healthy eating habits	2.23	0.62	2.24	0.74	0.09@
17.	Usage of electronic gadgets disturbs children sleeping pattern	2.80	0.48	3.19	0.77	2.33*
18.	Electronic gadgets play an important role in making children adapt to technological trends	2.97	0.55	2.83	0.47	1.07@
19.	Computer based games diminish the time spent on indoor activities	1.81	0.65	1.79	0.77	0.07@
20.	Electronic gadgets have lots of fun things to keep children entertained	3.23	0.50	3.00	0.38	2.02*
21.	Electronic gadgets have lots of educational content that teaches important lessons	2.97	0.41	2.97	0.50	0.02@
22.	Schools with digital class rooms improves quality of education	3.13	0.56	3.24	0.58	0.76@

* Significant at 0.05 level

@ Not Significant

The above table shows that out of 24 items, perceptions of undergraduate and postgraduate teachers did not differ significantly on 21 items. Same as mothers, undergraduate teachers have more positive perceptions that gadget usage is helpful for children's *attention, concentration and entertainment* than post graduate teachers. Same like post graduate mothers, post graduate teachers perceived gadget usage causes *sleeping disturbances* among children.

The Null Hypothesis Stated: *"Teachers' education has no effect on their perceptions towards children usage of electronic gadgets"*. The results demonstrated that undergraduate teachers perceived gadgets are helpful for their children whereas postgraduate teachers expressed health issues towards gadget usage. Hence the null hypothesis could be rejected.

It is evident from the findings that both mothers and teachers have positive perceptions towards gadget usage of preschool children. However they both raised concerns about health issues and content monitoring. Preschool teachers suggested that parents and children need to develop healthy media usage habits. As adult content and porn videos are widely available in the internet, parents should aware of parental control tools and monitoring strategies.

SCCOE (Santa Clara County Office of Education) report (2016) stated that "teachers, parents, health providers and child development experts all agree that the media children use can have a profound impact – both positive and negative – on learning, social development and behavior. Technology is also an integral component of schools today and applying the sensible recommendations of experts in medicine and education can increase the likelihood of positive outcomes".

Suggestions of Teachers towards Children Usage of Electronic Gadgets

Teachers influence not only children but also parents. If preschool teachers are knowledgeable on experts recommended screen time for preschool children, they can educate children and parents. Figure 4.14 depicts teachers' awareness on recommended screen time of preschool children.

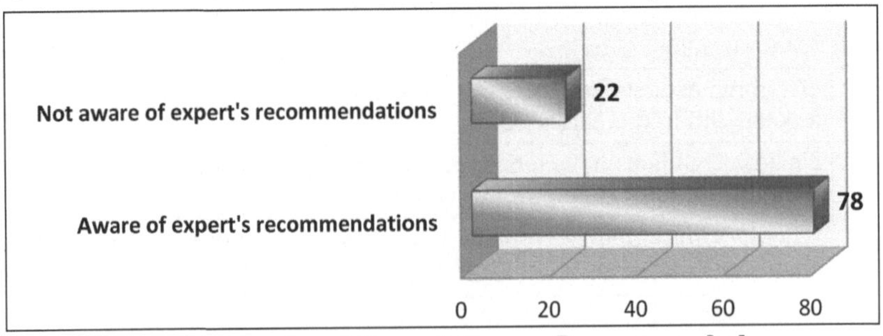

Fig. 4.14: Teachers' Knowledge on Recommended Screen Time for Preschool Children (N=60)

It is evident from the above figure that majority (78%) of preschool teachers have knowledge of experts recommended screen time for young children. Twenty two percent of teachers are not aware of experts' recommendations. Early childhood teachers need to have awareness on positive and negative impact of children screen time so that they can educate parents and children.

In order to understand teachers' preferred programmes for their students to watch, the data was arranged in the rank order based on the obtained total scores. The least possible score is 60 and highest possible score is 180 and the finding presented in the below table.

Table 4.27: Programs Teachers Prefer their Students to Watch (N=60)

Programme	Total Score	Rank Order
Educational programs/activities	159	1
Music	150	2
Cartoons	132	3
Games	130	4
Videos	104	5

The findings from the above table reveal that teachers given first preference to 'educational programmes' for their students to watch. Second preference is given to *music,* followed by *cartoon channels, games* and *videos.*

The choice of teachers is almost similar with mothers. Mothers have given second preference to cartoons and third preference to music while teachers' choice was in the reversal order for these two. For the remaining 3 options, teachers and mothers preferences are similar.

For the question *"effect of usage of electronic gadgets on children"*, majority (80%) teachers mentioned that gadget usage creates negative impact on preschool children and 65% stated that it causes health problems like attention disorders, obesity, visual problems, anxiety disorders etc. Fifteen percent of teachers reported that children may get addicted to electronic gadgets in the future. Contradicting to this, 47% preschool teachers opined that gadgets are useful for children to gain knowledge and 27% of them expressed that children can learn vocabulary and improve their language skills. Exactly one fourth (25%) said that children should be updated with technological trends and 18% stated that when children use gadgets, they will be updated with current issues.

Table 4.28: Teachers' Suggestions on Children Usage of Electronic Gadgets (N=60)

Effect of Usage of Electronic Gadgets on Children		
	Number	Percentage
Usage of gadgets has negative impact on children	48	80
Gadgets cause health problem in children	39	65
Gadgets are useful for children	28	47
Children learn new vocabulary and improve language skills	16	27
Children should be updated with technological trends	15	25
Children will be updated with current issues	11	18
Children may get addicted in the future	9	15
Reasons for Increased Usage of Electronic Gadgets by Children		
Dual earning families/parents are busy	45	75
Lot of attractive features and apps which attract children	40	67
As parents are using, children are imitating them	29	48
Entertainment	27	45
Availability and easy access of gadgets	24	40
Due to increased nuclear families	14	23
Lack of play area at home	11	18
Parents are not sending children out for play due to security reasons	9	15
Comparing with peers and others	7	12
Suggestions for Parents to Engage Children during Free Time		
Parents need to play with their children	42	70
Can take them for outings like parks, super markets, zoo etc.	41	68
Daily conversation between parents and children	31	52
Parents need to regulate their gadget usage timings as children imitate them	29	48
Teach moral values through stories	23	38
Have family meal time without gadgets	17	28
Involve children in the household tasks	8	13
Suggestions to Engage Children during Parental Absence		
Provide variety of indoor games	51	85
Engage children in the outdoor play	36	60
Engage children with book reading	34	57
Join them in activity/hobby classes	31	52

(Table Contd...)

The Role of Home in Regulating Children on Usage of Electronic Gadgets		
Regulate children usage timings and educate them	39	65
Parents need to monitor their children usage and content	35	58
Parents need to spend quality time with children and divert them	31	52
Protect the gadgets by keeping passwords	14	23
The Role of School in Regulating Children on Usage of Electronic Gadgets		
Educate children about advantages and disadvantages of usage	39	65
Provide them interesting home assignments	28	47
School needs to educate parents on how to regulate children usage	21	35

One third (75%) teachers expressed that dual earning families and parents' busy schedule are the main *reasons for increased usage of electronic gadgets by children"*. Sixty seven percent preschool teachers mentioned that gadgets are available with lot of features and apps which attract children. About half (48%) teachers stated that parents are role models to children and as parents are using the gadgets, children are also using by seeing them. Forty five percent expressed that gadgets entertain children and 40% mentioned that gadgets are available in the market with lower prices. Preschool teachers reported that due to increased nuclear families (23%) and lack of play area at home (18%), the time spent with gadgets by children has been increased. Fifteen percent teachers opined that parents are not sending children for outdoor play due to security reasons and as a result, children are spending more time with gadgets. Twelve percent of them reported that children are getting influenced by peer group and using gadgets.

The third question is *"Suggestions for parents to engage their children during free time"* Most of the teachers (70%) mentioned that parents need to engage children with play and divert them from the gadgets. Sixty eight percent of them answered that parents should take children to new places so that children will be explored to new things and acquire knowledge. Around half (52%) of the teachers wrote that parents need to communicate with children on daily basis and 48% of them suggested that parents must regulate their gadget usage time and spend time with children. Thirty eight percent expressed that parents need to teach moral values to children by telling stories and giving real life examples. Twenty eight percent teachers wrote that family meal time without gadgets is essential and 13% of them said that parents can involve children in the household works.

The next question is *"Suggestions to engage children during parents' absence"*. For this question, majority (85%) teachers suggested that children can be engaged with different indoor games like puzzles, blocks, board games etc and 60% of them said that children should be engaged with outdoor games which are helpful for their gross motor skills. More than half (57%) teachers mentioned that children need to be engaged with book reading habit. Fifty two percent teachers suggested that parents can join children in different hobby classes.

The fifth question is "*The role of home in regulating children on usage of electronic gadgets*". Majority (65%) of preschool teachers answered that parents need to regulate children usage time and they have to explain why children should not spend longer hours with gadgets. Similarly 58% teachers mentioned that parents have to monitor the content regularly. Around half (52%) of the teachers stated that parents should spend quality time with children and divert them from the gadgets. Twenty three percent teachers suggested that parents can protect the gadgets by creating passwords and keeping in the child safe mode.

To the question "*The role of school in regulating children on usage of electronic gadgets*", 65% teachers mentioned that school administration and teachers should educate children on the advantages and disadvantages of usage. Forty seven percent teachers opined that children should be provided with interesting and innovative home assignments so that it regulates their usage time. Thirty five percent teachers expressed that school needs to educate parents on how to engage children in better ways.

Thus it can be concluded from the above data that majority of the teachers expressed negative impact on gadget usage. They mentioned that due to parents' busy schedule, present generation kids are spending lot of time with gadgets. Preschool teachers suggested that parents need to regulate timings and monitor the content carefully. They opined that school should play an important role and educate parents and children on gadget usage.

LANGUAGE DEVELOPMENT OF PRESCHOOL CHILDREN

Preschool children's language skills are essential for their social interactions and academic success. During the early years of life, children learn to master in phonetics, vocabulary of words and grammar. Language enables children to express their needs with others and to participate in cultural learning in remarkable ways. Pre-literacy and literacy activities can help further children's language competencies in both the preschool years and later schooling.

Chomsky (1975) believed that children are born with an inherited ability to learn any human language. He claims that certain linguistic structures which children use so accurately must be already imprinted on the child's mind. Chomsky mentioned that every child has a 'language acquisition device' (LAD) which encodes the major principles of a language and its grammatical structures into the child's brain. Chomsky's theory applies to all languages as they all contain nouns, verbs, consonants and vowels and children appear to be 'hard-wired' to acquire the grammar.

Early learning is very critical in children's language development in both receptive and productive linguistic skills. Language acquisition through exposure is what is occurring in this stage of human life, where the language seeps into the child's mind unconsciously (Christakis, 2009).

Age and Language Development of Preschool Children

To assess language development of preschool children in the present study, nine language development tests were carried out and the obtained mean scores of 3-4 years, 4-5 years and 5-6 year old children are presented in the table 4.29.

Table 4.29: Means, SDs and 't' Values of 3-4, 4-5 and 5-6 Year Old Children on Language Development Tests (N=200)

Language Development Tests	Age	N	Mean	SD	't' value	
Following directions	3 to 4	85	4.04	1.56	3-4 & 4-5	2.02*
	4 to 5	39	4.64	1.55	4-5 & 5-6	2.61**
	5 to 6	76	5.38	1.21	3-4 & 5-6	6.15**
Following prepositions	3 to 4	85	3.45	1.24	3-4 & 4-5	2.10*
	4 to 5	39	3.99	1.38	4-5 & 5-6	2.05*
	5 to 6	76	4.53	1.22	3-4 & 5-6	5.57**
Naming and use of objects	3 to 4	85	7.20	1.42	3-4 & 4-5	1.47@
	4 to 5	39	7.56	1.21	4-5 & 5-6	1.96*
	5 to 6	76	7.95	0.22	3-4 & 5-6	4.78**
Naming and identification of objects	3 to 4	85	7.06	1.78	3-4 & 4-5	2.41*
	4 to 5	39	7.82	1.57	4-5 & 5-6	2.09*
	5 to 6	76	8.41	1.10	3-4 & 5-6	5.86**
Action agent test	3 to 4	85	7.79	2.37	3-4 & 4-5	1.09@
	4 to 5	39	8.31	2.50	4-5 & 5-6	2.72**
	5 to 6	76	9.47	1.31	3-4 & 5-6	5.67**
Comprehension test	3 to 4	85	7.25	4.57	3-4 & 4-5	2.92**
	4 to 5	39	9.92	4.80	4-5 & 5-6	3.47**
	5 to 6	76	12.93	3.52	3-4 & 5-6	8.89**
Ability to give name, age, sex and address	3 to 4	85	3.05	0.94	3-4 & 4-5	4.28**
	4 to 5	39	3.92	1.11	4-5 & 5-6	3.08**
	5 to 6	76	4.53	0.72	3-4 & 5-6	11.29**

(Table Contd...)

Language Development Tests	Age	N	Mean	SD	't' value	
Ability to distinguish AM, PM, Right and Left	3 to 4	85	3.33	1.37	3-4 & 4-5	1.18@
	4 to 5	39	3.64	1.37	4-5 & 5-6	3.20**
	5 to 6	76	4.42	0.94	3-4 & 5-6	5.93**
Indication of parts of the body	3 to 4	85	5.53	1.97	3-4 & 4-5	1.02@
	4 to 5	39	5.90	1.82	4-5 & 5-6	1.77@
	5 to 6	76	6.50	1.55	3-4 & 5-6	3.49**

* Significant at 0.05 level
** Significant at 0.01 level
@ Not Significant

From the above table it observed is that when the age increases, children scores on language tests have increased significantly. Out of 9 languages tests, 5-6 years age group children scored higher in all tests than 3-4 year old children. Among 9 language tests, 5-6 years age group children scored higher than 4-5 year old children on 8 language tests except indication of parts of the body test.

The findings also indicate that out of 9 language tests, 4-5 year age group children scored higher on 5 tests – following directions, following prepositions, naming and identification of objects, comprehension test and ability to give name, age, sex and address test as compared to 3-4 year old children.

In the ***following directions*** test, 5-6 year old age group children scored higher than 4-5 years and 3-4 years, 4-5 year old age group children scored higher than 3-4 year children. This test contains 3 sub tests where children need to place the objects according to the directions. Comparatively, elder age group i.e. 5-6 year children completed the task with ease than younger group i.e. 4-5 and 3-4 year old children.

The second language test is ***following prepositions*** and in this test, 5-6 year children scored higher as compared to 4-5 year and 3-4 year old children and 4-5 year old children scored higher than 3-4 year old children. Six prepositions – on, in, behind, under, in front, beside were tested in this category. UKG children i.e. children belong to 5-6 years were able to understand maximum number of prepositions when compared with LKG and Nursery children. Most of younger age group i.e. 3-4 year old children could not understand prepositions like behind and beside.

In the ***naming and use of objects*** test, elder age group i.e. 5-6 year old children scored higher than 4-5 years and 3-4 year children. In this test, 4 objects were shown to children and asked them to give the name and use of those objects. Almost all children were able to name the objects but comparatively 5-6 year old children explained the use of objects than 4-5 year and 3-4 year children. Elder children have shown clear vocabulary while explaining the use of objects. Grabmeier (2012) emphasized the preschool teacher's role in promoting reading and language skills of children. He suggested that simple steps like pointing out letters and words, showing capital letters and how to read text from left to right and from top of the side to bottom will stimulate children reading skills.

The ***naming and identification of objects*** test contains 5 picture cards. In this test, 5-6 year age group children scored higher than 4-5 years and 3-4 year old children and 4-5 year old children scored higher as compared to 3-4 year children. Children were asked to name the objects in the picture cards. If they can not name the object, names were given and asked them to identify the objects. Majority of children performed well in this test but younger children consumed more time in completing the task when compared with elder age group.

In the ***action agent test,*** 5-6 year age group scored higher than 4-5 year and 3-4 year old children. This test contains 10 picture cards and each card has 2 pictures. Children need to identify the correct picture based on the action given. Children enjoyed doing this test and 5-6 year old children completed this test with ease. Most of the Nursery children i.e. 3-4 year old children took longer time to complete the task as compared to 4-5 years and 5-6 years.

The ***comprehension test*** includes 4 questions where children need to explain solutions to the problems. Five to six year old age group children scored higher than 4-5 years and 3-4 years and 4-5 year age group children scored higher than 3-4 year old children. Five to six year old children have given clear explanations with examples to the questions whereas younger children had explained in broken sentences. According to Mol and Bus (2011), children who are read to more frequently at an early age enter school with larger vocabularies and more advanced comprehension skills.

In the ***ability to give name, age, sex and address*** test, 5-6 year age group children scored higher than 4-5 and 3-4 year old children. Similarly 4-5 year old children scored higher than 3-4 year age group. In this test children need to tell their name, age, gender and address. Higher age group children were able to tell their name, age and gender. When it comes to address, most of 5-6 year old children could name the city and area but 3-4 year age group could not do so.

The ***ability to distinguish AM, PM, Right and Left*** test contains 5 questions. Elder group i.e. 5-6 year old children scored higher than 4-5 and 3-4 year old children in this test. Almost all children answered to three questions – "what do you do in the morning, afternoon and night?" But only few 5-6 and 4-5 year old children were able to identify right and left. When compared with 3-4 and 4-5 year children, 5-6 year age group children took less time to complete the test.

The ninth test is ***indication of parts of the body*** and in this test, 5-6 year old children scored higher than 3-4 year old children. This test has 9 questions in which children need to show nine parts of their body. Majority of children were able to show 6 to 7 body parts out of 9. Younger age group i.e. 3-4 and 4-5 years faced difficulty in showing palm and knees. Comparatively, 5-6 year age children completed the test faster than younger children.

Thus it can be concluded from the above results that elder age group i.e. 5-6 years children have higher language skills than younger age groups i.e. 4-5 and 3-4 years. Likewise 4-5 year old children have shown better language skills than 3-4 year old children. Umek and Peklaj (2017) findings from their meta-analysis indicated small gender differences in language ability which, however increased with children's increasing age.

Gender and Language Development of Preschool Children

Subsequently gender is another factor to study the influence on language development. In a research, Wilsenach and Makaure (2018) found that girls performed significantly better than boys on all the reading measures, as well as on some aspects of phonological processing. The findings provide behavioural evidence in support of biological theories of gender differences, in that girls seemed to have developed some of the cognitive-linguistic skills associated with reading before boys. Table 4.30 shows mean scores of boys and girls on language development tests.

Table 4.30: Means, SDs and 't' Values of Boys and Girls on Language Development Tests (N=200)

S.No.	Language Tests	Boys (N=119)		Girls (N=81)		't' Value
		Mean	SD	Mean	SD	
1.	Following directions	4.55	1.57	4.84	1.51	1.33@
2.	Following prepositions	3.83	1.35	4.22	1.33	2.02*
3.	Naming and use of objects	7.52	1.18	7.60	1.03	0.53@
4.	Naming and identification of objects	7.65	1.48	7.83	1.81	0.74@
5.	Action agent test	8.39	2.35	8.73	1.93	1.10@
6.	Comprehension test	9.41	4.88	10.81	5.01	1.96*
7.	Ability to give name, age, sex and address	3.63	1.09	3.95	1.15	1.98*
8.	Ability to distinguish AM, PM, Right and Left	3.67	1.37	4.05	1.22	2.04*
9.	Indication of parts of the body	5.73	1.93	6.32	1.63	2.33*

* Significant at 0.05 level

@ Not Significant

It is evident from the findings that out of 9 language tests, boys and girls differed significantly on 5 tests. Among all these five tests, girls scored higher on *following prepositions, comprehension test, ability to give name, age, sex and address, ability to distinguish AM, PM, Right and Left, indication of parts of the body* tests than boys. It was observed that girls had clear pronunciation, vocabulary and communication compared with boys. Comparatively girls took lesser time in completing the language tests. Bornstein *et.al.* (2004) found in their study that, in the second through fifth year of age but not before or after, girls expressed higher language ability than boys of the same age.

The findings of several studies on gender differences in language development suggest that girls develop language faster than boys. Erikson report (2016) stated that girls are found to speak earlier, acquire the grammar of the language faster, use longer utterances and express a larger vocabulary throughout infanthood, toddlerhood and early childhood.

Umek and Peklaj (2017) found that parents used more symbolic transformations when playing with girls than with boys, thus providing more opportunities for the girls to engage in symbolic play, which is largely supported by the use of language and strongly related to more advanced language ability in children. The figure 4.15 illustrates the mean scores of boys and girls on language development tests.

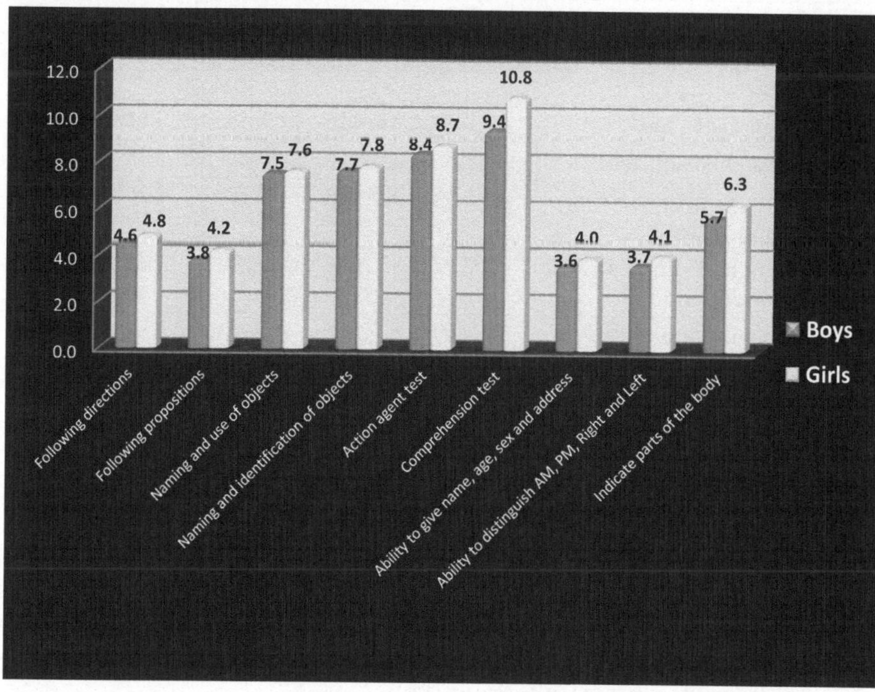

Fig. 4.15: Mean Scores of Boys and Girls on Language Development Tests

The above figure shows that girls scored higher on language development tests when compared with boys.

Usage of Electronic Gadgets and Language Development of Preschool Children

Usage of technology is an important aspect which influences language development of children. Krcmar *et.al.* (2007) stated that technology has become part of the child's immediate environment as well, and its influence on language is undeniably significant. Their study found that children can effectively learn vocabulary from videos associated with live social interactions. Means, SDs and t values on language development tests of low gadget usage and high gadget usage children on a typical working day is presented in table 4.31.

Table 4.31: Means, SDs and 't' Values on Language Development Tests of Low and High Gadget Usage Children during Working Day

S.No.	Language Tests	Low Gadget Usage Children (N=95)		High Gadget Usage Children (N=40)		't' Value
		Mean	SD	Mean	SD	
1.	Following directions	4.38	1.61	4.98	1.48	2.08*
2.	Following prepositions	3.94	1.34	3.90	1.50	0.13@
3.	Naming and use of objects	7.51	1.08	7.40	1.45	0.41@
4.	Naming and identification of objects	7.72	1.70	7.60	1.52	0.39@
5.	Action agent test	7.40	3.26	8.55	1.81	2.09*
6.	Comprehension test	9.67	5.00	10.25	5.35	0.58@
7.	Ability to give name, age, sex and address	3.80	1.08	3.73	1.20	0.34@
8.	Ability to distinguish AM, PM, Right and Left	3.92	1.23	3.55	1.66	1.25@
9.	Indication of parts of the body	6.00	1.86	5.68	1.99	0.88@

* Significant at 0.05 level

@ Not Significant

The findings reveals that out of 9 language tests, children with low gadgets usage and high gadget usage during working day differed significantly on two tests. Children with high gadget usage during working day scored higher in the *following directions test* and *action agent test* when compared with low gadget usage children. Figure 4.16 represents the mean scores of language development tests of low gadget usage and high gadget usage children on a typical working day.

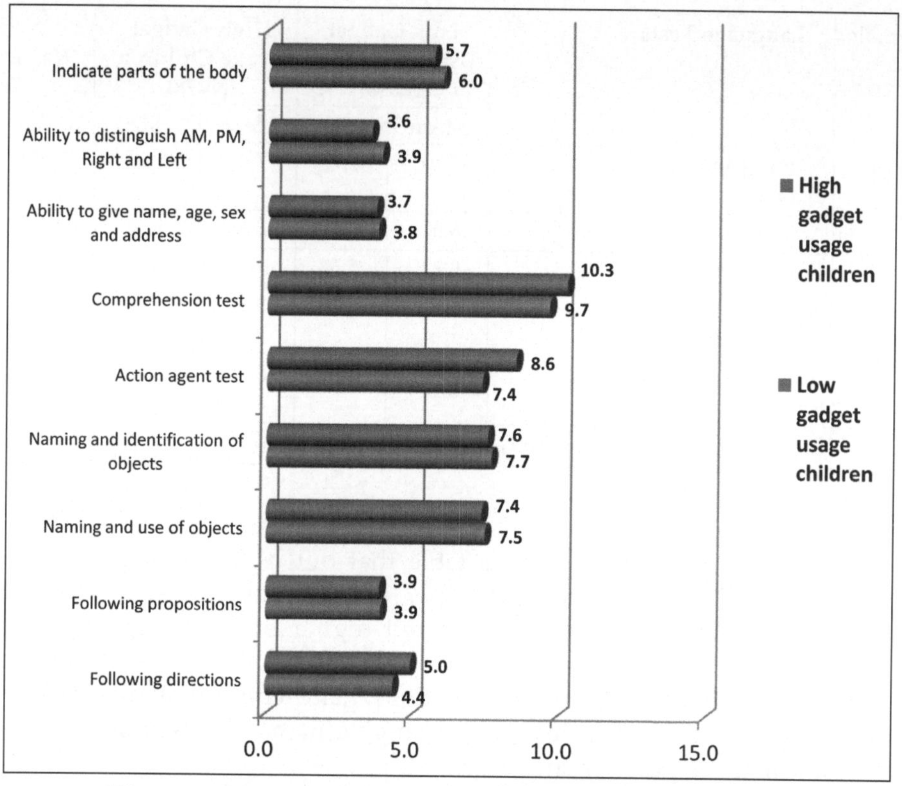

Fig. 4.16: Mean Scores on Language Development Tests of Low and High Gadget Usage Children on a Working Day

Some studies revealed that children watching interactive and educational content would enhance their language development. Anderson etal (2001) study found that watching educational programs designed to engage children, like Sesame Street, can have a beneficial effect for preschool age children because they can comprehend and learn from such programs.

Means, SDs and t values on language development tests of low gadget usage and high gadget usage children during holiday is presented in table 4.32.

Table 4.32: Means, SDs and 't' Values on Language Development Tests of Low and High Gadget Usage Children during Holiday

S.No.	Language Tests	Low Gadget Usage Children (N=58)		High Gadget Usage Children (N=78)		't' Value
		Mean	SD	Mean	SD	
1.	Following directions	4.22	1.72	4.78	1.47	1.99*
2.	Following prepositions	3.60	1.31	4.10	1.31	2.20*
3.	Naming and use of objects	7.22	1.36	7.69	1.00	2.21*

(Table Contd...)

S.No.	Language Tests	Low Gadget Usage Children (N=58)		High Gadget Usage Children (N=78)		't' Value
		Mean	SD	Mean	SD	
4.	Naming and identification of objects	7.50	1.97	7.81	1.25	1.05@
5.	Action agent test	8.07	2.51	8.88	2.10	1.99*
6.	Comprehension test	8.72	5.63	10.58	4.94	2.00*
7.	Ability to give name, age, sex and address	3.52	1.13	3.91	1.11	2.02*
8.	Ability to distinguish AM, PM, Right and Left	3.69	1.31	3.78	1.45	0.39@
9.	Indication of parts of the body	5.48	2.01	6.19	1.75	2.14*

* Significant at 0.05 level
@ Not Significant

It is evident from the above table that out of 9 language tests, the two groups differed significantly on 7 tests. Among these seven tests, children with high gadget usage scored higher on language tests than children with low gadget usage during holiday. These 7 tests include following directions, following prepositions, name and use of objects, action agent test, comprehension test, ability to give name, age, sex and address and indication of parts of the body.

Figure 4.17 represents the mean scores of language development tests of low gadget usage and high gadget usage children during holiday.

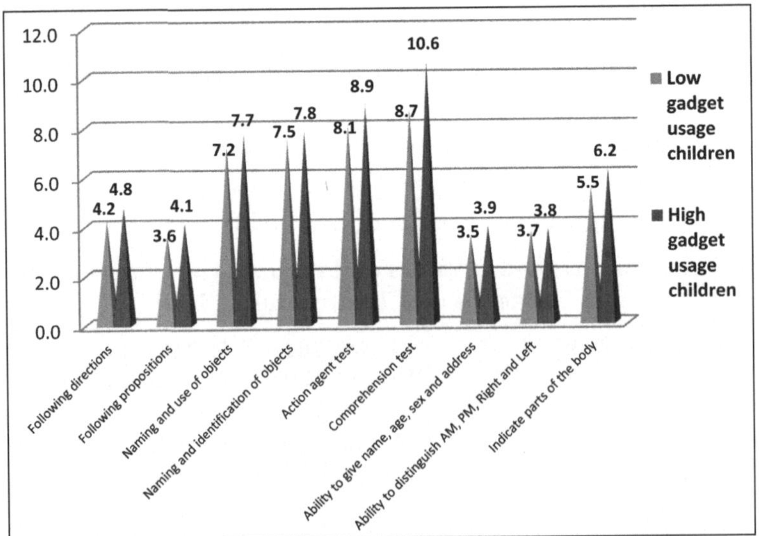

Fig. 4.17: Mean Scores on Language Development Tests of Low Gadget Usage and High Gadget Usage Children during Holiday

The Null Hypothesis Stated: *"Low and high electronic gadget usage preschool children do not differ significantly on their language development"*. Based on the findings of the present study, high gadget usage children scored higher on language development tests on both working day and holiday than low gadget usage children. Thus the null hypothesis could be rejected.

In a study, Gibbons (2009) mentioned that 'children with many reading experiences from various media and from environments where the parents were involved in their reading activities, have a higher phonological consciousness, broader knowledge of letters, and a more extensive vocabulary compared to children who do not get this support'. So the role of parents is a key factor for the language acquisition of children. To understand the influence of parents usage of electronic gadgets on their children's language development, mean, SDs and t values were calculated and the results are presented in table 4.33.

Table 4.33: Means, SDs and 't' Values on Language Development Tests of Children of Low and High Gadget Usage Parents

S.No.	Language Tests	Children of low gadget usage mothers (N=71)		Children of high gadget usage mothers (N=56)		't' Value
Mother's Usage						
		Mean	SD	Mean	SD	
1.	Following directions	4.65	1.56	4.50	1.56	0.53@
2.	Following prepositions	3.92	1.34	3.77	1.29	0.64@
3.	Naming and use of objects	7.55	1.13	7.70	0.87	0.82@
4.	Naming and identification of objects	7.70	1.61	7.68	1.31	0.08@
5.	Action agent test	8.52	2.20	8.89	1.66	1.09@
6.	Comprehension test	9.88	4.95	10.09	4.83	0.24@
7.	Ability to give name, age, sex and address	3.77	1.11	3.84	1.07	0.35@
8.	Ability to distinguish AM, PM, Right and Left	3.80	1.32	3.82	1.28	0.09@
9.	Indication of parts of the body	5.95	1.83	6.13	1.57	0.58@
Father's Usage						
S.No.	**Language Tests**	**Children of low gadget usage fathers (N=45)**		**Children of high gadget usage fathers (N=91)**		**'t' Value**
		Mean	**SD**	**Mean**	**SD**	
1.	Following directions	5.00	1.49	4.60	1.56	1.43@
2.	Following prepositions	3.78	1.36	4.09	1.31	1.26@

(Table Contd...)

3.	Naming and use of objects	7.36	1.40	7.69	0.84	1.49@
4.	Naming and identification of objects	8.00	1.22	7.78	1.42	0.93@
5.	Action agent test	8.47	2.26	8.74	1.97	0.68@
6.	Comprehension test	9.84	4.90	10.41	4.84	0.63@
7.	Ability to give name, age, sex and address	3.60	1.14	3.88	1.09	1.36@
8.	Ability to distinguish AM, PM, Right and Left	3.73	1.50	3.84	1.25	0.39@
9.	Indication of parts of the body	6.11	1.75	5.95	1.81	0.52@

* Significant at 0.05 level;

@ Not Significant

The findings from the above table indicate that children of low gadget usage and high gadget usage mothers differ significantly on none of the nine language tests. Hence it is found that mother's usage of electronic gadgets did not create an impact on child's language development.

Similarly, the results showed that children of low and high gadget usage fathers did not differ significantly on any of the nine language tests. Consequently father's usage of electronic gadgets also did not influence language development of preschool children.

Honig (2007) stated that caregivers and teachers are crucial supporters for oral language flowering. Since the social context is so critical for rich oral language acquisition, parents and teachers need to become aware of their own understandings about how language is organized and what the different aspects of language are. These meta-linguistic skills permit talk about all rules, aspects and stages of language development.

Barr and Wyss (2008) found that parents who scaffolded their infants' television viewing experience by asking questions and commenting, had children who were more likely to pay attention and interact with the program. Over time, it was speculated that children would internalize these interactions and engender a cognitively active viewing approach to television which lead to better narrative comprehension.

It can be concluded from the present section that when the age increases, language development of 3 to 6 year old children has been increased significantly. Preschool girls scored higher on all language tests as compared to boys. The results found that children with high gadget usage scored higher on language development tests than children with low gadget usage. Parents' usage of electronic gadgets did not influence the language development of children. Thus it can be assumed that gadget usage create positive impact on language development of children. When children watch different educational programs, videos, rhymes etc they will pick up new vocabulary and improve their language skills.

SOCIAL SKILLS AND PROBLEM BEHAVIOUR OF PRESCHOOL CHILDREN

Social Skills of Preschool Children

The early years of a child's life play a vital role in the development of young children in shaping their socio-emotional skills. It depends on a variety of factors such as physical health, mental health and environmental conditions etc. These factors can have both positive and negative influence on children's development. Children who experience positive relationships at the early years will create positive influence on their social development in the later stages.

Children learn social rules, communication strategies and the encoding and decoding of emotional information from their parents. Theoretical models of social skill development suggest that parents and the family environment significantly impact a child's social development (Beauchamp and Anderson, 2010).

Age and Social Skills of Preschool Children

Social skills predict children's academic competence, self-esteem and school adjustment (Ray and Elliott, 2006). Furthermore, children who begin school with poorly developed social skills are more likely to be rejected by their peers, exhibit externalizing problems, and struggle with academics (McClelland etal, 2000). Hence it is important to assess social skills of children and the present section deals with social skills of 3 to 6 year old children. The table presented below shows the distribution of children as per their age and functional level of social skills.

Table 4.34: Distribution of Children as per their Age and Functional Level of Social Skills (N=200)

Social Skills	Functional Level	3-4 years (N=85)		4-5 years (N=39)		5-6 years (N=76)		X^2 test
		N	%	N	%	N	%	
Social cooperation	High	30	35.3	20	51.3	41	53.9	14.81*
	Average	45	52.9	17	43.6	33	43.4	
	Moderate deficit	8	9.4	1	2.6	1	1.3	
	Significant deficit	2	2.4	1	2.6	1	1.3	
Social interaction	High	34	40.0	22	56.4	47	61.8	22.10**
	Average	36	42.4	14	35.9	28	36.8	
	Moderate deficit	13	15.3	2	5.1	1	1.3	
	Significant deficit	2	2.4	1	2.6	0	0.0	
Social independence	High	30	35.3	18	46.2	38	50.0	14.13*
	Average	39	45.9	17	43.6	35	46.1	
	Moderate deficit	9	10.6	2	5.1	1	1.3	
	Significant deficit	7	8.2	2	5.1	2	2.6	

* Significant at 0.05 level

** Significant at 0.01 level

Merrill defined "***social cooperation*** is a form of social interaction wherein two or more persons work together to gain a common end". The above table shows that the obtained chi-square value on social cooperation of 3-4, 4-5 and 5-6 year age groups is 14.81. So there is significant association between age and social cooperation functional levels. As the age increases, children play together, they share their toys with others and cooperate with adults.

A research demonstrated that children begin to engage in pro-social or helping behaviors in their preschool age, sharing toys with parents, and other adults and cooperating with adults and peers to perform a goal (Warneken and Tomasello, 2006).

Dawson and Gettyes defined ***social interaction*** as "a process by which men interpenetrate the minds of each other". The chi-square value on social interaction of the above 3 age groups is 22.10 which is more than the table value and significant at 0.05 level. This describes that there is association between age and social interaction functional levels.

Burdette *et.al* (2005) reported in their study that "well-designed outdoor play environments will provide the necessary structure to support social interactions, creating an important place where children can learn social skills through play".

Building ***Social independence*** is part of an individual's social skills and self-reliance allows the child to feel they have control over their life. The acquired chi-square value of age and social independence is 14.13 which demonstrates that there is association between age and functional levels of social independence. When the age increases, children will learn to be independent, they will be able to mingle with others easily, can make friendships, separate from their parents without distress and they will enjoy group activities.

As the above chi-square values are significant, it can be concluded that there is considerable association between age and social skills of preschool children. The present results are in line with the findings of Klarin (2016) study which showed increased social behaviour between four to six year old age group children.

The figure 4.18 demonstrates distribution of children as per their age and functional levels of social skills.

The results reveal that majority of children in the above age groups scored high and average functional levels of social skills and less than one fourth children scored moderate and significant deficit function levels.

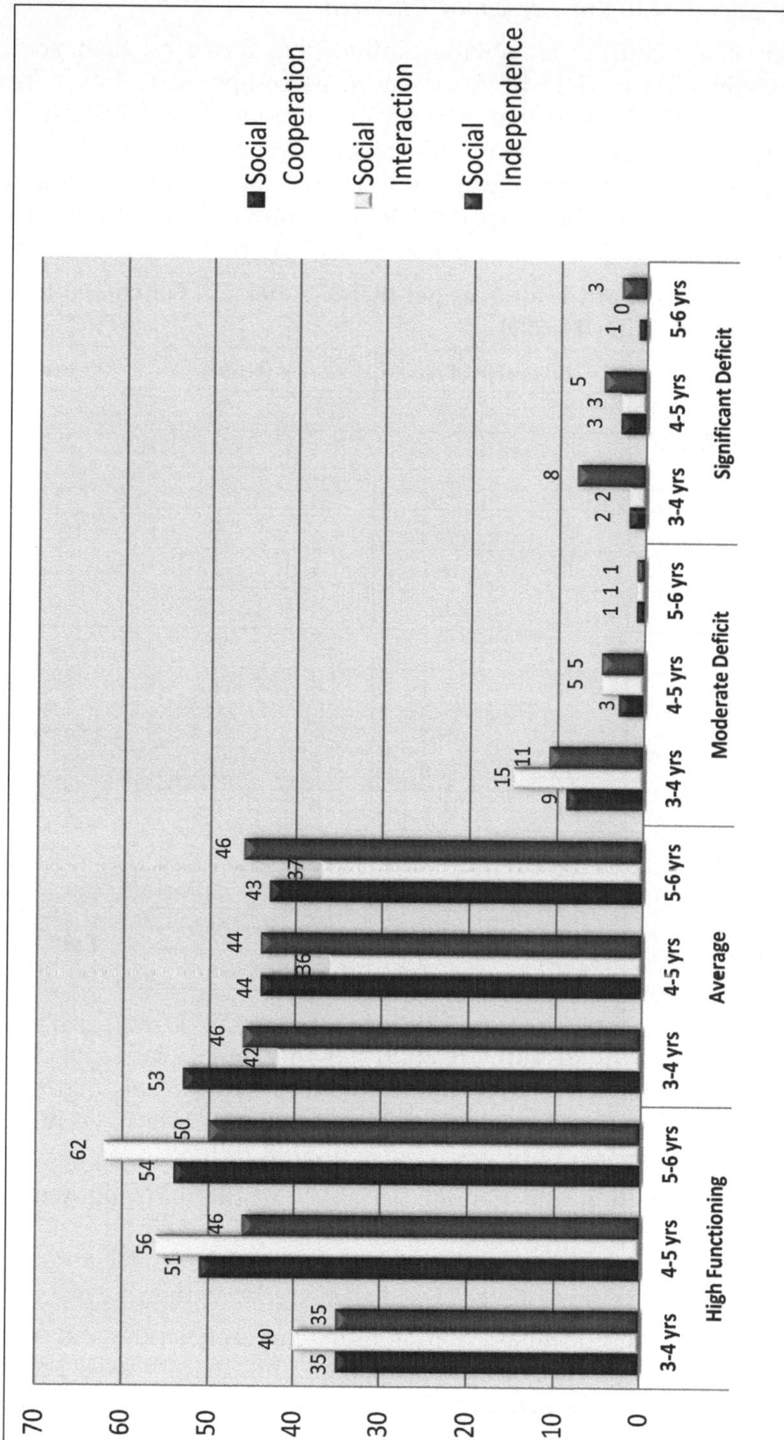

Fig. 4.18: Distribution of Children as per their Age and Functional Levels of Social Skills

Gender and Social Skills of Preschool Children

Gender of the child is an obvious influencing factor on their social skills. Generally girls tend to be more social as compared to boys. In a study, Sonja *et.al.* (2009) found that girls exhibited more desired social skills like peer relation, self management and academic behaviour than the boys whereas boys scored higher than girls on undesired social skills like hostile, aggressive and disruptive behaviour. Table 4.35 shows the distribution of children as per their gender and functional level of social skills.

Table 4.35: Distribution of Children as per their Gender and Functional Level of Social Skills (N=200)

Social Skills	Boys (N=119)		Girls (N=81)		X^2 test
	N	%	N	%	
Social Cooperation					
High functioning	44	37.0	45	55.6	9.02*
Average	58	48.7	33	40.7	
Moderate deficit	12	10.1	3	3.7	
Significant deficit	5	4.2	0	0.0	
Social Interaction					
High functioning	37	31.1	49	60.5	17.93***
Average	63	52.9	23	28.4	
Moderate deficit	15	12.6	9	11.1	
Significant deficit	4	3.4	0	0.0	
Social Independence					
High functioning	39	32.8	42	51.9	9.89*
Average	53	44.5	31	38.3	
Moderate deficit	15	12.6	3	3.7	
Significant deficit	12	10.1	5	6.2	

The obtained chi-square value of child's gender and social cooperation is 9.02. It is higher than the table value at 0.05 level and reveals that there is association between gender and social cooperation. Girls have higher functioning level of social cooperation as compared to boys.

On social interaction and gender variables, results have shown the obtained chi-square value as 17.93 which is significant at 0.05 level. Hence it is found that there is association between gender and social interaction. Girls have higher functioning level of social interactions than boys.

Same as above, significant association found between gender and social independence. For these variables, the obtained chi-square 9.89 is greater than the table value at 0.05 level of significance. Therefore it is noticed that comparatively girls have higher social independence than boys.

Thus it can be concluded from the above findings that girls scored higher on social cooperation, social interaction and social independence as compared to boys. These results are in line with a recent study (Hinkley *et.al.*, 2018) which showed that girls had significantly higher scores on social skills than boys of 2 to 5 year old age group. The below figure depicts the distribution of children as per their gender and functional levels of social skills.

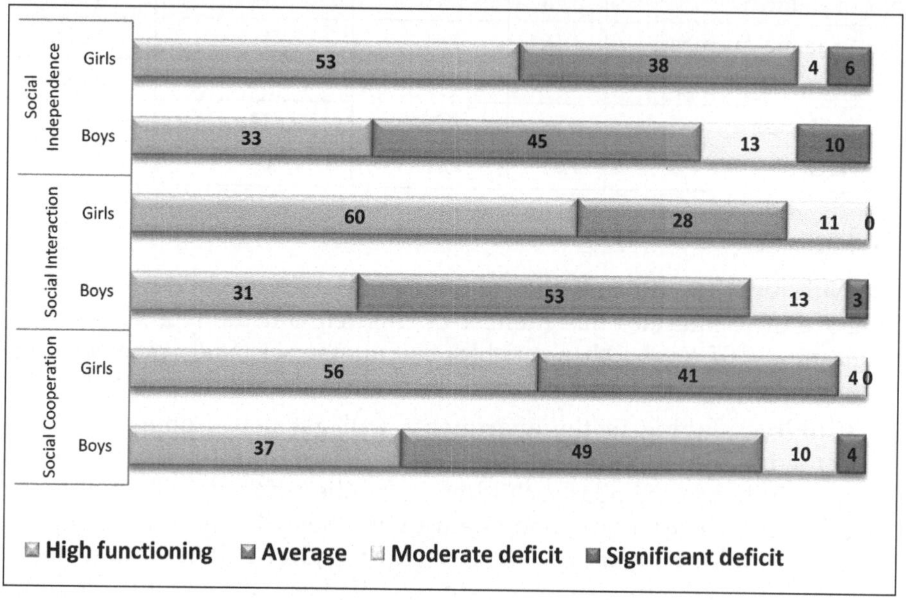

Fig. 4.19: Distribution of Children as per their Gender and Functional Levels of Social Skills

The findings of Fivush (2000) study explained the reasons for the higher social skills of girls. In his study, he found that mothers are more consistently emotionally expressive than fathers and express more positive emotions with their daughters than their sons thereby modeling such behaviors to their children.

Usage of Electronic Gadgets and Social Skills of Preschool Children

There are many socializing agents that influence social skills of children such as child's family, neighborhood, school etc. To examine the influence of family variables on social skills, regression analysis is carried out and the results are presented in table 4.36.

Table 4.36: Influence of Family Variables on Child's Social Skills

Coefficients				
Variable	Unstandardized Coefficients		Standardized Coefficients	't' value
	B	Std. Error	Beta	
No. of children	3.78	2.19	.14	1.98*
No. of family members	1.16	1.11	.11	1.04@
Type of family	1.73	1.79	.09	0.96@
Type of house	3.83	2.29	.12	1.97*
Play area	1.54	2.76	.04	0.56@

* Significant at 0.05 level

@ Not Significant

With regard to the influence of family variables on child's social skills, the above table indicates that number of children and the type of house are significant at 0.05 level. Other variables like number of family members, type of family and play area do not significantly affect the child's social skills.

Children staying in the apartments will get better opportunities to interact with other children as compared to children staying in the independent houses. Similarly, children in families with more than one child will get more chances to play and interact with their siblings when compared with single child. In a study, Downey and Condron, (2004) found that at the beginning of kindergarten, single children are exhibiting fewer interpersonal skills, less self-control and greater externalizing problem behaviors than children with at least one sibling.

In the contemporary society, another important factor which influences a child's social skills is technology. The amount of time child and parents spend with electronic gadgets would create an impact on their social skills. Drago's (2015) findings suggest that technology has a negative effect on both the quality and quantity of face-to-face communication. In the present study, means, SDs and 't' values on social skills of low and high gadget usage children on a typical working day is presented in the table 4.37.

Table 4.37: Means, SDs, 't' Values on Social Skills of Low and High Gadget Usage Children on a Typical Working Day

Social Skills	Low Usage (N=95)		High Usage (N=40)		't' value
	Mean	SD	Mean	SD	
Social Cooperation	31.91	4.62	29.23	7.47	2.11*
Social Interaction	27.65	4.83	25.05	7.27	2.08*
Social Independence	28.65	4.74	26.28	6.98	1.96*

* Significant at 0.05 level

The results from the above table reveal that children with low gadget usage and high gadget usage on a working day differed significantly on 3 social skills subscales – social cooperation, social interaction and social independence. Among these subscales, children with low gadget usage scored higher than the children with high gadget usage on a working day. Thus it is evident that children with low gadget usage are having higher levels of social skills than children with high gadget usage. The below figure represents the mean scores on social skills of low and high gadget usage children during working day.

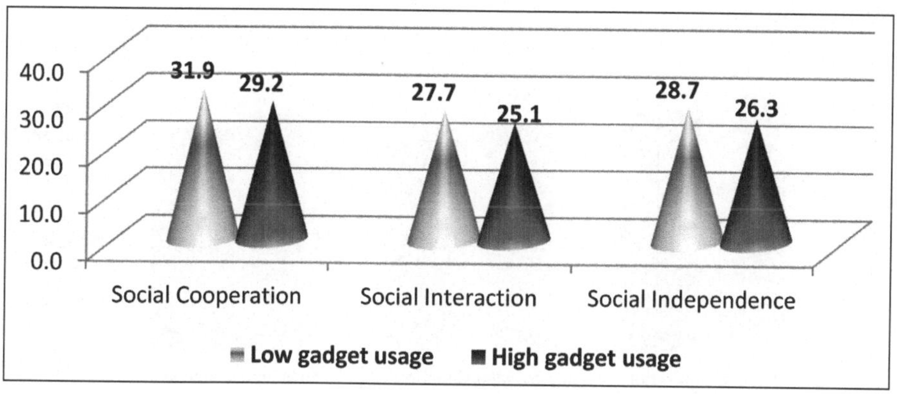

Fig. 4.20: Mean Social Skills Scores of Low and High Gadget Usage Children during Working Day

Studies have shown that children those who spend less time with gadgets and more time with family and friends will develop social skills. According to Radesky *et.al* (2015), social and emotional skills are learned through regular social interactions and screen media can interrupt these essential early interactions. They suggested that time spent watching TV displaces time which would be spent on early social interactions and that inadequate social skills may develop because of this displacement. The table presented below shows means, SDs and t values on social skills of low and high gadget usage children during holiday.

Table 4.38: Means, SDs, 't' Values on Social Skills of Low and High Gadget Usage Children during holiday

Social Skills	Low Usage (N=58)		High Usage (N=78)		't' value
	Mean	SD	Mean	SD	
Social Cooperation	32.15	4.82	30.08	7.37	1.98*
Social Interaction	28.40	4.84	26.14	6.81	2.26*
Social Independence	29.28	4.58	27.33	6.50	2.04*

* Significant at 0.05 level

Similar results found with regard to usage electronic gadgets during holiday. The above table shows that the two groups differed significantly on all three subscales i.e. social cooperation, social interaction and social independence. The results reveal that children with low gadget usage scored higher on social skills than high gadget usage children during holiday. Bhattacharya (2015) stated that the effect of gadget usage excessively will raise interpersonal and communication skill problem in children and it will take them away from nature and surrounding environment. The below figure shows the mean scores on social skills of low and high gadget usage children during holiday.

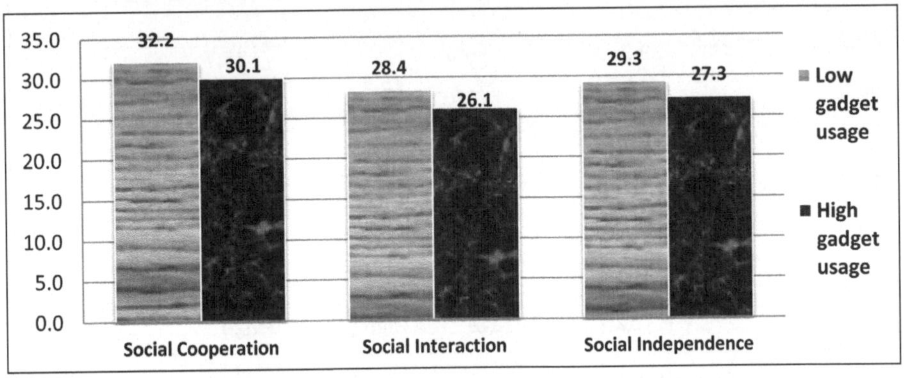

Fig. 4.21: Mean Scores on Social Skills of Low and High Gadget Usage Children during Holiday

It can be seen from the above figure that high gadget usage children scored lower on social cooperation, social interaction and social independence than low gadget usage children during holiday.

The Null Hypothesis Stated: *"Low and high electronic gadget usage preschool children do not differ significantly on their social skills"*. The findings of the present study reveal that low electronic gadget usage children scored higher social skills as compared with high gadget usage children on both working day and holiday. Hence the null hypothesis could be rejected.

Bickham, *et.al.* (2006) investigated the relationship between TV viewing time, content, context and peer integration. As children spend more total time watching TV, they spend a significantly shorter amount of time with friends as compared to those who don't. Thus, viewing television causes poor peer relationships and thereby increases the risk for social isolation, anxiety disorder, agoraphobia, and antisocial behavior, including aggression and gang involvement.

Bukato (2008) reported in his study that television is consuming much of child's time, with passively and daily viewing television programmes, children are less engaged with people such as parents and siblings.

Consequently, children are finding it increasingly difficult to interact and relate with peers given that the family unit forms the basis of all other future relationships.

Since preschool children spend maximum time with their parents, it is important to understand parents' electronic gadget usage time and its influence on children's social skills. Table 4.39 represents the regression analysis of child, mother and father's usage of electronic gadgets and child's social skills.

Table 4.39: Influence of Child's, Mother's and Father's Usage of Electronic Gadgets on Child's Social Skills

Coefficients				
Model	Unstandardized Coefficients		Standardized Coefficients	't' value
	B	Std. Error	Beta	
Child's usage	1.39	0.49	0.21	2.82**
Father's usage	0.66	0.48	0.11	1.38@
Mother's usage	0.89	0.39	0.19	2.23*

* Significant at 0.05 level

** Significant at 0.01 level

@ Not Significant

With regard to the influence of child's, mother's and father's usage of electronic gadget on social skills, the above table indicates that child's usage of electronic gadgets has significant impact on their social skills at 0.01 level and mother's usage of electronic gadgets has significant impact on child's social skills at 0.05 level of significance. Whereas, father's usage of electronic gadgets did not significantly affect the social skills of children. Table 4.40 refers mean, SDs and t values on social skills of children of low electronic gadget usage and high electronic gadget usage parents.

Table 4.40: Means, SDs and 't' Values on Social Skills of Children of Low and High Gadget Usage Parents

Mother's Usage						
S.No.	Social Skills	Children of low gadget usage mothers (N=71)		Children of high gadget usage mothers (N=56)		't' Value
		Mean	SD	Mean	SD	
1.	Social cooperation	34.93	6.35	31.59	6.67	2.86*
2.	Social interaction	29.93	6.13	27.66	6.52	2.00*
3.	Social independence	26.90	6.39	25.38	6.74	1.29@

(Table Contd...)

Father's Usage						
S.No.	Social Skills	Children of low gadget usage fathers (N=45)		Children of high gadget usage fathers (N=91)		't' Value
		Mean	SD	Mean	SD	
1.	Social cooperation	30.13	6.43	31.20	6.76	0.89@
2.	Social interaction	25.76	6.38	27.12	6.36	1.17@
3.	Social independence	26.84	6.29	28.14	5.92	1.15@

The results as appearing in the above table show that out of 3 social skills subscales, children of low and high gadget usage mothers differed significantly on 2 subscales. Children of low gadget usage mothers scored higher on social cooperation and social interaction when compared with children of high gadget usage mothers. In contrast, children of low and high gadget usage fathers did not differ significantly on the above three social skills subscales.

Preschool children spend most of the time with their mothers when compared with fathers. So mothers' spending time with gadgets influences on their children's social skills. Ralston (2015) stated that distracted parenting as being a direct threat to child's welfare as parents are often more engaged in their devices as opposed to supervising their children closely. Vandewater *et.al* (2006) found that the more time children spent watching television, the less time they spent with their families.

Gani (2016) reported the negative effect invoked by gadget is child's social skill development. He mentioned that 'child will lack in interaction with environment, parents and peers. The child's habit of playing gadget will result dependency behavior which can destruct child's social and emotional development and leads to lack of socialization in the community. This socialization process will be continued from childhood to adulthood'.

It can be concluded from the present section that there is significant association between preschool children age, gender and their social skills. Social skills of the children increased with the increase of age. Girls scored higher on social cooperation, social interaction and social independence than boys. Children who are spending less time with electronic gadgets during working day and holiday scored higher on social skills as compared with the children who are spending more time with gadgets. The results are also evident that mothers' usage of electronic gadgets significantly influence the social skills of preschool children.

Problem Behaviour of Preschool Children

Some sort of naughtiness and disobedient behavior is common among young children. However some children exhibit exceptionally difficult behaviours which is challenging for the parents and teachers to handle. Common behaviour problems during preschool stage are aggression, temper tantrums, defiance, eating problems, sleeping problems, impulsiveness, whining etc. Early diagnosis, intervention and behaviour modifying strategies are crucial for controlling the problematic behaviour.

A child's behavioral problems represent a conflict between his developing personality and that of his parents, teachers, siblings and of other children with whom he comes into contact (Mainiero and Sullivan 2005). Behavior problems in young children are common and usually load on two major dimensions described as internalizing (withdrawal, fearfulness, sadness, somatic problems) and externalizing (hyperactivity, inattention, aggression, defiance) factors (Achenbach, 1991).

A study conducted on behavior problems among preschool children in New Delhi revealed that 22% of them had behavioral problems (Rai *et.al*, 1993). Studies conducted in developed countries have shown that child conduct or behavior problems have negative impacts on children's social, educational and economic performance in later life (Fergusson *et.al*, 2005). Thus there is a need to understand the problem behaviour of preschool children.

Age and Problem Behaviour of Preschool Children

Age is assumed to be an obvious predictor to assess the influence on problem behaviour of preschool children. The table presented below shows the distribution of children as per their age and functional level of problem behaviour.

Self-centeredness means excessive concern about one's own self and *explosive* behaviour includes anger, violence and impulsiveness. The obtained chi-square value on self-centeredness of 3-4, 4-5 and 5-6 year age groups is 23.54 which is greater than the table value and significant at 0.05 level. It indicates that there is association between age and self-centeredness functional levels. So it can be observed that there is increase in the self-centeredness with increase in the age. Similar results are found in Morine *et.al* (2011) research which revealed that the incidence of aggression in preschool students is noticeably greater at age four than at age three. Social learning theorist Bandura (1973) explained that children learn social behaviors including aggression and relational styles within family relationships, which they then use with friends and peers.

Attention problem/overactive behaviour problem children show difficult in concentrating on one particular task, disrupting the activities, impulsive acts without thinking, hyper-activeness etc. A research demonstrated that parent anxiety disorders increase the risk for similar problems in children. Parent anxiety symptoms moderated the relationship between parent and child externalizing symptoms such that the strength of this relationship was reduced in the presence of high levels of parent and children anxiety symptoms (Burstein, 2010). In the present study, no association is found between age and attention problem/overactive behavior among preschool age children.

Table 4.41: Distribution of Children as per their Age and Functional Level of Problem Behaviour (N=200)

Problem Behaviour	Functional Level	3-4 years (N=85)		4-5 years (N=39)		5-6 years (N=76)		X^2 test
		N	%	N	%	N	%	
Self-centered/ Explosive	No Problem	55	64.7	18	46.2	34	44.7	23.54*
	Average	29	34.1	20	51.3	41	53.9	
	Moderate Problem	1	1.2	1	2.6	1	1.3	
	Significant Problem	0	0	0	0	0	0	
Attention Problem/ Overactive	No Problem	44	51.8	28	71.8	57	75.0	8.91@
	Average	38	44.7	10	25.6	18	23.7	
	Moderate Problem	3	3.5	1	2.6	1	1.3	
	Significant Problem	0	0	0	0	0	0	
Antisocial/ Aggressive	No Problem	56	65.9	24	61.5	44	57.9	10.66*
	Average	24	28.2	15	38.5	30	39.5	
	Moderate Problem	5	5.9	0	0	1	1.3	
	Significant Problem	0	0	0	0	1	1.3	
Social Withdrawal	No Problem	51	60.0	22	56.4	42	55.3	1.71@
	Average	27	31.8	15	38.5	32	42.1	
	Moderate Problem	3	3.5	1	2.6	2	2.6	
	Significant Problem	4	4.7	1	2.6	0	0	
Anxiety/Somatic Problem	No Problem	61	71.8	26	66.7	45	59.2	18.23*
	Average	20	23.5	12	30.8	29	38.2	
	Moderate Problem	4	4.7	1	2.6	2	2.6	
	Significant Problem	0	0	0	0	0	0	

* Significant at 0.05 level
@ Not Significant

The *anti-social* behaviours are actions that harm or lack consideration for the wellbeing of others. Patterson and Fisher (2002) found in their study that negative parenting including verbal criticism, parent-child conflict and harsh discipline has been robustly associated with antisocial behavior problems in children. The obtained chi-square value of age and anti-social/ aggressive behaviour is 10.66 which shows that the association is significance at 0.05 level. The results reveal that anti-social/aggressive behaviour can be seen more in elder age group children than younger children.

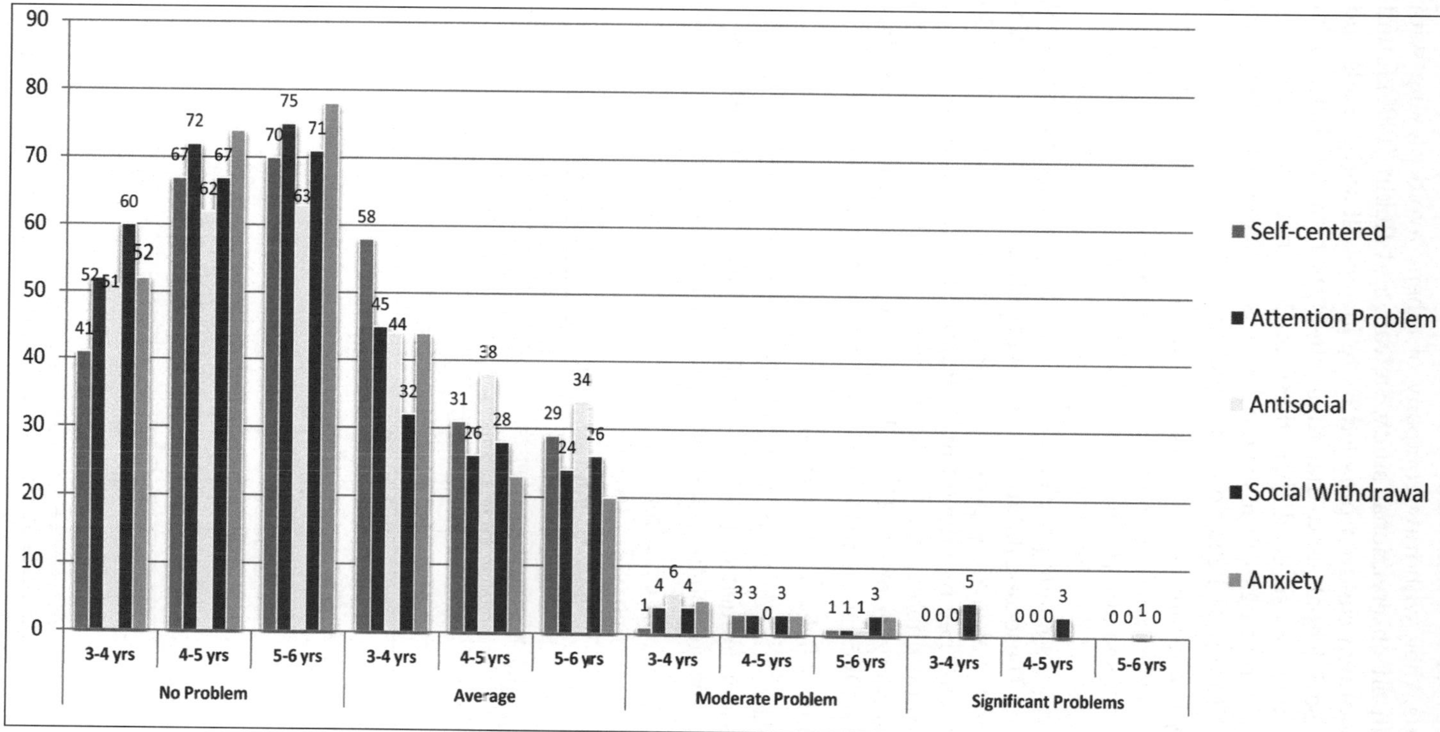

Fig. 4.22: Distribution of Children as per their Age and Functional Levels of Problem Behaviour Scores

Thus it is can be noticed from the above results that elder age group children i.e. 5-6 year age group scored higher on self-centeredness, anti-social behaviour and anxiety problems when compared with the younger age group children i.e. 4-5 years and 3-4 year old children.

Children with ***social withdrawal*** behaviour problem will have problems in making friends, they withdraw company of others, avoid playing with other children. In an observational study, Stewart and Rubin (1995) found that socially withdrawn children pursued more lower-cost social goals and fewer high-cost social goals and that their attempts to meet their social goals were less likely to succeed than those of their non-withdrawn age mates. The present findings disclose that there is no association between age and social withdrawal behaviour of children.

The ***anxiety*** is a feeling of worry, fear or distress and ***somatic problem*** includes physical ache, pain or sickness. The calculated chi-square values on age and anxiety/somatic problem is 18.23 which is more than the table value and significant at 0.05 level. Five to six year age group children have shown more anxiety/somatic problems than four to five and three to four year old children. These results are in line with Bhatia and Goyal (2018) study which found that anxiety problems are more in older children than younger age groups. They mentioned the common anxiety disorders among children are specific phobia, social phobia, generalized anxiety disorder, and separation anxiety disorder. The below figure depicts the distribution of children as per their age and problem behaviour functional levels.

Gender and Problem Behaviour of Preschool Children

Child's gender is a key factor that influences the behaviour of children. To study the gender influence on child's problem behaviour, an attempt is made to calculate the chi-square values and the data is presented in table 4.42.

Table 4.42: Distribution of Children as per their Gender and Functional Level of Problem Behaviour (N=200)

Problem Behaviour	Boys (N=119)		Girls (N=81)		X^2 test
	N	%	N	%	
Self-centered/Explosive					
No Problem	67	56.3	49	60.5	
Average	48	40.3	32	40.5	1.93@
Moderate Problem	4	3.4	0	0	
Significant Problem	0	0	0	0	
Attention Problem/Overactive					
No Problem	76	63.9	53	65.4	
Average	37	31.1	25	30.9	1.94@
Moderate Problem	3	2.5	3	3.7	
Significant Problem	3	2.5	0	0	
Antisocial/Aggressive					
No Problem	67	56.3	51	63.0	
Average	47	39.5	27	33.3	1.38@
Moderate Problem	4	3.4	3	3.7	
Significant Problem	1	0.8	0	0	

(Table Contd...)

Social Withdrawal					
No Problem	70	58.8	50	61.7	2.25@
Average	39	32.8	27	33.3	
Moderate Problem	7	5.9	2	2.5	
Significant Problem	3	2.5	2	2.5	
Anxiety/Somatic Problem					
No Problem	78	65.5	54	66.7	0.11@
Average	34	28.6	23	28.4	
Moderate Problem	7	5.9	4	4.9	
Significant Problem	0	0	0	0	

@ Not Significant

It is evident from the results that there is no significant association between the gender and behaviour problem subscales. So it can be assumed that preschool girls and boys show similar pattern of self-centeredness, attention problems, anti-social behaviour, social withdrawal and anxiety problems.

Usage of Electronic Gadgets and Problem Behaviour of Preschool Children

In recent society, electronic media is integrated into the lives of adults, children and even the youngest age group. The American Academy of Pediatrics recommends no more than 2 hours per day of screen time for preschool children and no screen time for children under the age of 2 with screen time defined as time spent using or watching televisions, computers, phones and other electronic devices (Committee on Public Education, 2001).

A longitudinal study that tracked New Zealand youth between the ages of 5 and 15 found increased television exposure in childhood leading to increased attention problems in the teenage years (Landhuis *et.al*, 2007). Hence there is need to know the relation between children usage of electronic gadgets and their problem behaviour pattern. The table 4.43 represents the means, SDs and t values on problem behaviour of low gadget usage children and high gadget usage children during working day.

Table 4.43: Means, SDs, 't' Values on Problem Behaviour of Low and High Gadget Usage Children on a Typical Working Day

Problem Behaviour	Low Usage (N=95)		High Usage (N=40)		't' value
	Mean	SD	Mean	SD	
Self-centered/Explosive	3.92	4.04	6.10	6.10	2.08*
Attention Problem/Overactive	3.35	4.11	5.52	6.46	1.96*
Antisocial/Aggressive	1.45	2.50	2.72	3.71	1.97*
Social Withdrawal	1.56	2.68	3.18	4.35	2.18*
Anxiety/Somatic Problem	2.32	3.13	3.93	4.14	2.21*

* Significant at 0.05 level

It can be observed from the above table that children with low electronic gadget usage and high gadget usage on a typical working day differed significantly on all the five behaviour problem subscales – *self-centered/explosive, attention problem/overactive, antisocial/aggressive, social withdrawal* and *anxiety/somatic problems.* High electronic gadget usage children scored higher on problem behaviour as compared to children with low gadget usage. Thus it reveals that high gadget usage leads to behaviour problems among preschool children. The figure 4.23 represents the mean scores on problem behavior of low and high gadget usage children during working day.

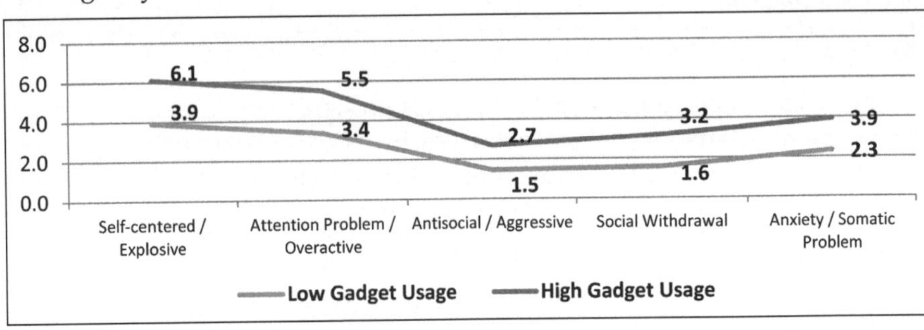

Fig. 4.23: Mean Problem Behaviour Scores of Low and High Gadget Usage Children during Working Day

These results are in line with the findings of Griffiths *et.al,* (2010) study which revealed that using screen entertainment for more than 2 hours a day is associated with emotional and conduct problems in five year old children. In another study, Daly and Perez (2008) examined whether viewing television violence is associated with aggression in preschool children during spontaneous play in USA and results showed that violent TV content was associated with preschool children's aggressive behavior.

Means, SDs and t-values on problem behaviour of low and high gadget usage children during holiday are presented in the table 4.44.

Table 4.44: Means, SDs, 't' Values on Problem Behaviour of Low and High Gadget Usage Children during Holiday

Problem Behaviour	Low Usage (N=58)		High Usage (N=78)		't' value
	Mean	SD	Mean	SD	
Self-centered/Explosive	4.07	4.54	5.79	5.72	1.96*
Attention Problem/Overactive	3.62	4.43	5.39	5.93	2.00*
Antisocial/Aggressive	1.71	2.62	2.82	3.93	1.98*
Social Withdrawal	1.69	3.17	2.80	3.31	1.97*
Anxiety/Somatic Problem	2.62	3.58	3.86	3.55	1.99*

* Significant at 0.05 level

Same as working day results, the above table shows that children with low and high gadget usage during holiday differed significantly on *self-centered/explosive, attention problem/overactive, antisocial/aggressive and social withdrawal* subscales. Children with high gadget usage scored higher on all the above scales when compared with low gadget usage children. The below figure illustrates the mean scores on problem behaviour of children with low and high gadget usage during holiday.

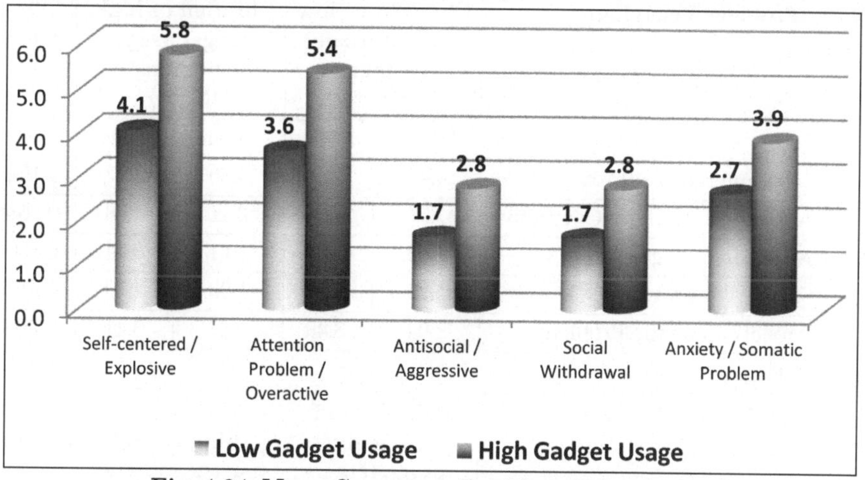

Fig. 4.24: Mean Scores on Problem Behaviour of Low and High Gadget Usage Children during Holiday

It can be concluded from tables 4.43 and 4.44 that children with high electronic gadget usage scored higher in the problem behaviour than low gadget usage children. Similar results were found in a recent study conducted by Hosokawa and Katsura (2018) which shown that preschool gadget users spending 60 minutes or more a day had significantly more behaviour problems and symptoms (i.e., conduct problems, hyperactivity/ inattention, and emotional symptoms) compared to non-users or users spending less than 60 minutes on a typical day.

The Null Hypothesis Stated: *"Low and high electronic gadget usage preschool children do not differ significantly on their problem behaviour"*. The null hypothesis could be rejected as per the results of the present study. High electronic gadget usage children scored higher on problem behaviour as compared to low electronic gadget usage children.

Manivannan *et.al* (2017) assessed the knowledge of mothers on children behaviour problems. They found that 61% of mothers have inadequate knowledge, 37% of mothers have moderately adequate level of knowledge and only 2% of mothers have adequate knowledge on behavior problems of children. They suggested that multi-level community based interventions targeting peers, parents, teachers and community leaders could be a feasible and acceptable approach to address the identify problems.

In order to understand the parental usage of electronic gadgets and its influence on their children's problem behaviour, means, SDs and 't' values were calculated and the results are presented below.

Table 4.45: Means, SDs and 't' Values on Problem Behaviour of Children of Low and High Gadget Usage Parents

Mother's Usage						
S.No.	Problem Behaviour	Children of low gadget usage mothers (N=71)		Children of high gadget usage mothers (N=56)		't' Value
		Mean	SD	Mean	SD	
1.	Self-centered/Explosive	4.49	4.89	3.50	4.77	1.15@
2.	Attention Problem/Overactive	3.77	5.04	3.11	4.78	0.76@
3.	Antisocial/Aggressive	1.66	2.73	1.61	3.44	0.10@
4.	Social Withdrawal	2.27	3.53	1.98	2.79	0.51@
5.	Anxiety/Somatic Problem	3.04	3.49	2.57	3.41	0.76@
Father's Usage						
S.No.	Problem Behaviour	Children of low gadget usage fathers (N=45)		Children of high gadget usage fathers (N=91)		't' Value
		Mean	SD	Mean	SD	
1.	Self-centered/Explosive	5.27	5.25	4.08	5.19	1.25@
2.	Attention Problem/Overactive	4.20	4.67	3.98	5.47	0.25@
3.	Antisocial/Aggressive	1.91	2.97	1.91	3.38	0.00@
4.	Social Withdrawal	2.44	3.59	1.79	2.81	1.07@
5.	Anxiety/Somatic Problem	3.07	3.48	2.37	3.26	1.12@

The above table shows that children of low and high gadget usage mothers did not differ significantly in any of the five problem behaviour subscales. It means mothers' usage of electronic gadgets did not influence their children's problem behaviour pattern.

Similarly there is no significant difference found with children of low gadget usage and high gadget usage fathers with respect to the above five problem behaviour subscales. Hence it is found that fathers' usage of electronic gadgets also did not create an impact on children's problem behaviour.

The findings of present section reveal that there is association between age and problem behaviour of preschool children. In contrast, there is no association between gender and problem behaviour of children. Children with high electronic gadgets usage scored higher on problem behaviour subscales than low gadget usage children on both working day and holiday. The results also reveal that parental usage of electronic gadgets did not influence their children's problem behaviour.

As preschool children's high gadget usage is associated with their problem behaviour, parents need to regulate the electronic gadget usage of children. Children can be engaged with activities like indoor and outdoor games, art and craft activities, puzzles, building blocks, story books etc to reduce the screen time.

5

Summary and Conclusion

The present study explored the usage of electronic gadgets, language development, social skills and problem behaviour among preschool children. The research also aimed to study the perceptions of mothers and teachers towards children usage of electronic gadgets.

The study was conducted in Hyderabad city, Telangana State. Eleven private preschools were selected randomly from total number of 1146 schools. To find out the availability of Television, Smart phone, Computer, Laptop, Tablet/Ipad, Game console in the families, a checklist was prepared and sent to all 680 parents from those 11 schools. After careful scrutiny of the forms, 391 families were found to be suitable for the present study as they have 4 out of 6 electronic gadgets. By using simple random sampling technique, 200 mothers and 200 children were selected for the final sample. The sample also consists of 60 preschool teachers from eleven preschools.

The following tools were used for collecting the data:

1. Availability and Usage of Electronic Gadgets Questionnaire
2. Perceptions of Mothers towards Children Usage of Electronic Gadgets Questionnaire
3. Perceptions of Teachers towards Children Usage of Electronic Gadgets Questionnaire
4. Language Development Tests (LDT)
5. Preschool and Kindergarten Behaviour Scales (PKBS2)

Availability and Usage of Electronic Gadgets Questionnaire contains 13 items in the first section (Background information of the subjects) and 15 items in the second section (Availability and usage of electronic gadgets), total number of 28 items are included. Test re-test reliability of the tool is 0.78.

Perceptions of Mothers towards Children Usage of Electronic Gadgets Questionnaire consists of 31 items. The first section "mothers' perceptions" includes 24 statements with 2 point continuum – Agree or Disagree options. The second section "suggestions of mothers" consists of 7 questions which include both open-ended and closed-ended. Test-retest reliability is 0.89 and Guttman Split-half reliability is 0.73.

Perceptions of Teachers towards Children Usage of Electronic Gadgets Questionnaire includes 30 questions – first section (teachers' perceptions) has 22 statements and second section (suggestions of teachers) consists of 8 open-ended and closed-ended questions. Test-retest reliability is 0.86 and Guttman Split-half reliability is 0.73.

Language Development Tests used in this study were taken from NCERT publications (1986). These language tests were adapted from Gesell Scale and modified to the Indian standards. In the present study, few modifications were done by reframing four questions to suit the current trend. Cronbach's alpha reliability of the tool is 0.86.

Preschool and Kindergarten Behaviour Scales (PKBS2) is a behavioural rating instrument for the use in evaluating social skills and problem behaviour of preschool and kindergarten aged children, aged three through six. It is a norm referenced, standardized instrument developed by Merrell (2002). The PKBS2 includes two major scales: *Social skills* (34 items) and *Problem behaviour* (42 items). The original form of PKBS has been shown to have excellent psychometric properties. The internal consistency coefficients are 0.87 for the social skills items (scale A), and 0.92 for the problem behaviour items (scale B). For the present study, Cronbach's alpha was calculated on 100 sample for norming the reliability suitable to Indian standards. The obtained value is .96 for social scale and .94 for problem behaviour scale which shows high internal consistency of the tool.

The data was collected from mothers in one session with an interval of 10 minutes between two questionnaires - Availability and usage of electronic gadgets questionnaire' and 'Perceptions of mothers towards children usage of gadgets questionnaires'. From preschool teachers, in one session, 'Perceptions of teachers towards children usage of electronic gadgets questionnaire' was given. For the second session, teachers who were handling selected preschool children for the final sample were gathered and 'Preschool and Kindergarten Behaviour Scale' was given. Language development tests were administered individually on preschool children. After data collection, the data was analyzed by using appropriate statistical methods. The following are major findings of the present study.

MAJOR FINDINGS

Usage of Electronic Gadgets:

- The results reveal that almost all families (99%) are having television set and 15% of them are having more than one television set at home. Similarly, all families (99.5%) are having smartphones and 86.5% of them have more than one smart phone. More than half (54.5%) of the families are having computers and around 77% of them have laptops. Nearly half (51%) of the families are having tablets and 17% are having game consoles at home.
- The findings show that 23.5% of preschool children are having their own tablet/IPad and 10% of them are owned game consoles.
- The usage of electronic gadgets is high in 20% of preschool children during working day whereas it is almost doubled (39%) during holiday. Usage is low in 47.5% of children on a working day while it is low in 29% of children during holiday. Hence it is found that preschool children are spending more time with gadgets on holidays than working days.
- Significant association found between age and usage of electronic gadgets during holiday. Whereas no association found between age and usage of gadgets on a typical working day.
- The usage of electronic gadgets is high in 22% boys and 20% of girls on a typical working day. Whereas, usage is high in 45% of boys and 30% of girls during holiday. Thus it reveals that boys are spending more time with gadgets on a holiday as compared to girls.
- The findings indicate that *mothers' education* and *availability of play area at home* have significant impact on child's usage of electronic gadgets at 0.05 level of significance.
- With regard to the parental usage of electronic gadgets, 28% of mothers scored high in the usage of electronic gadgets whereas 45.5% of fathers scored high usage on a working day. Fathers are spending more time with electronic gadgets when compared with mothers.
- The results reveal that 10% of preschool children are using the gadgets throughout the day – before going to school, after reaching home, meal time and bed time. Most of the children are using gadgets during meal time and mothers have expressed that it helps to make them complete their meal faster.
- Majority of children are operating game apps in the gadgets, followed by videos, internet, camera and music features. The data also shows that a greater part of children are watching cartoons in the gadgets followed by educational programs, videos, games and music.

- The results are evident that one fourth (25%) of the parents do not regulate timings of children spending time with electronic gadgets. Whereas 32% of parents regulate the time for 1 hour per day, 19% of parents set 2 hours per day, 17% mothers restrict for half an hour and 7% set time for 3 to 4 hours per day. The findings also reveal that 56% of children show temper tantrums when parents regulate timings and 44% of children willingly switch off the devices.
- Majority of parents are allowing children to use gadgets *'during meal time'*, followed by *'when they are busy with household works'*. Next occasion is *'when they are busy with guests'* and parents engage children with gadgets *'while doing their office work at home'*. This is followed by the occasion wherein *'parents watch their favorite programmes'* and next occasion shows that *'when they go out'*, to engage their children parents provide gadgets.
- Almost all (98%) houses with preschoolers are equipped with toys. Seventy eight percent of families are having books, followed by games and sports (76%) material, indoor games like puzzles and building blocks (76%) and 67% of families have craft material available at home.
- More than half of children (53.5%) as well as mothers (60.5%) are very much interested in reading books. One third (34%) of children are not spending time with books at all. Majority (41.5%) of preschool children are spending time with books like story books, comics, picture books for half-an-hour in a day, 16% of them are spending for one hour and 7% of children are reading books for more than one hour in a day with the help of their parents.

Perceptions of Mothers:

- Mothers have expressed positive opinions towards children usage of electronic gadgets. Majority (81.5%) of mothers agreed with the statement *"electronic gadgets influence children to develop language skills"*. Eighty one percent of mothers agreed that *"electronic gadgets play an important role in making children adapt to technological trends"*. Eighty six percent of mothers opined that *"electronic gadgets have lots of fun things to keep children entertained"*.
- Contradicting to the above, mothers have perceived negative impact of gadget usage on preschool children. Almost all (97%) the mothers agreed up on the statement *"children's time with electronic gadgets reduces their outdoor play time"*. Majority of mothers (79.5%) have agreed with the statement *"electronic gadgets influence children to develop gender stereotypic behaviour"*. Eighty one percent of mothers accepted that *"electronic gadgets influence children to show aggressive and violent behaviour"*. Most of mothers (86.5%) perceived that *"children spending more time*

with electronic gadgets creates health problems in them such as obesity, visual problems etc". Majority (77%) of mothers perceived that *"usage of electronic gadgets disturbs children sleeping pattern"*.

- Some mothers expressed their concerns towards gadget usage of children. Eighty percent of mothers opined that *"commercial ads influence children to seek kids' products"*. Around three fourth (71.5%) of the mothers have expressed that *"I am concerned that my child may become addicted to electronic gadgets in the future"*. Majority (79%) of mothers agreed with the statement *"family's viewing of screen time has taken over the family time"*.
- Mothers of younger age group perceived that electronic gadgets influence children to develop language, reading and writing, social, cognitive skills and moral values. They also felt that gadgets are useful for developing children's attention and concentration. Mothers of above 30 year age group believed that gadget usage causes health problems and diminish the time spent on indoor activities like board games, puzzles, books etc. They also expressed concerns like gadget addiction and their children exposure to media during their absence.
- Undergraduate mothers perceived that usage of electronic gadgets is helpful for children to develop reading and writing skills, moral values, attention and concentration. While post graduate mothers opined that gadget usage leads to unhealthy eating habits and disturbance in sleeping pattern.
- Working mothers have positive perceptions that usage of gadgets is helpful for children's creativity and academic performance. In contrast, non-working mothers are more concerned that usage of gadgets create gender stereotypic behaviour among preschool children.
- Nearly three fourth (73%) of preschool mothers are aware of experts recommended screen time for their children. Whereas more than one fourth (27%) of the mothers do not have knowledge on experts recommendations.
- Around one third (35%) of mothers are spending 1-2 hours quality time with their children on a working day. Thirty one percent of mothers are spending 3-4 hours, one fourth (25%) of mothers are spending more than 4 hours with their children in a day.

  Few mothers (8.5%) agreed that they are able to spend less than one hour with their children on a working day.
- Majority (73%) of mothers mentioned that they play with their children every day. Sixty two percent of mothers shared that they tell stories to their children. Fifty six percent of mothers mentioned that they

help their children in completing the home works every day. Forty one percent of mothers shared that they take children to different places like shops, super markets, parks etc.

Perceptions of Teachers:

- Same as mothers, preschool teachers have mixed opinions towards children usage of electronic gadgets. Majority (95%) of teachers agreed with the statement *"electronic gadgets influence children to develop language skills"*. Nearly three fourth (73%) of teachers opined that *"electronic gadgets influence children to develop social skills"*. Ninety percent of preschool teachers agreed the statement *"electronic gadgets play an important role in making children adapt to technological trends"*. Majority (93%) of the teachers perceived that *"electronic gadgets have lots of educational content that teaches important lessons"*. Ninety two percent of teachers agreed with the statement *"schools with digital class rooms improve quality of education"*.
- Almost all (98%) early childhood teachers accepted that *"children's time with electronic gadgets reduces their outdoor play time"*. Ninety percent of teachers agreed with statements *"electronic gadgets influence children to develop gender stereotypic behaviour"* and *"electronic gadgets influence children to show aggressive and violent behaviour"*. Almost all (97%) teachers perceived that *"children spending more time with electronic gadgets creates health problems in them such as obesity, visual problems etc"*. Most of the teachers (92%) agreed that *"computer based games diminish the time spent on indoor activities like board games, puzzles, reading books etc"*.
- Below 30 year old age group teachers opined that gadgets are useful for children creative development and gadgets have lot of educational content that teaches important lessons to children. They have also perceived that schools with digital classrooms improve quality of education. Teachers above 30 years believed that usage of electronic gadgets is helpful for children to develop moral values, attention and concentration. They have raised concern about children sleeping disturbances because of screen time.
- Undergraduate teachers have more positive perceptions that gadget usage is helpful for children's attention, concentration and entertainment. Whereas post graduate teachers perceived gadget usage causes sleeping disturbances among children.
- Majority (78%) of preschool teachers have knowledge of experts recommended screen time for young children. Twenty two percent of teachers are not aware of experts' recommendations. Early childhood teachers need to have awareness on positive and negative impact of children screen time so that they can educate parents and children.

Language Development:

- The findings reveal that when the age increases, language development has been increased significantly.
- Out of 9 language tests, boys and girls differed significantly on 5 tests. Among all these five tests, girls scored higher on *following prepositions, comprehension test, ability to give name, age, sex and address, ability to distinguish AM, PM, Right and Left, indication of parts of the body* tests than boys.
- Children with low and high gadget usage during working day differed significantly on two language tests. Children with high gadget usage during working day scored higher in the *following directions test* and *action agent test* when compared with low gadget usage children.
- Similarly, children with high gadget usage scored higher on language tests than children with low gadget usage during holiday. These 7 tests include *following directions, following prepositions, name and use of objects, action agent test, comprehension test, ability to give name, age, sex and address and indication of parts of the body.*

Social Skills:

- The social skills scale consists of 3 subscales – social cooperation, social interaction and social independence. There is significant association between age and social skills of preschool children. Social skills of the children increased with their increase in age.
- Girls scored higher on social cooperation, social interaction and social independence as compared to boys.
- With regard to the influence of family variables on child's social skills, *number of children* and *type of house* have significant influence at 0.05 level.
- Children with low gadget usage and high gadget usage on a working day differed significantly on 3 social skills subscales – social cooperation, social interaction and social independence. Among these subscales, children with low gadget usage scored higher than the children with high gadget usage on a working day. Thus it is evident that children with low gadget usage are having higher levels of social skills than children with high gadget usage on a working day. In the same way, children with low gadget usage scored higher on social skills than high gadget usage children during holiday.
- Child's usage of electronic gadgets has significant impact on their social skills at 0.01 level and mother's usage of electronic gadgets has significant impact on child's social skills at 0.05 level of significance.

Problem Behaviour:

- The problem behaviour scale has 5 subscales – self-centered/explosive, attention problem/overactive, antisocial/aggressive, social withdrawal and anxiety/somatic problem. There is an association between age and problem behaviour of 3 to 6 year old children.
- In contrast, there is no association between gender and problem behaviour of preschool children.
- Children with low and high gadget usage on both working day and holiday differed significantly on all the five behaviour problem subscales. Children with high electronic gadget usage scored higher in the problem behaviour than low gadget usage children.

CONCLUSION

The results reveal that preschool children's usage of electronic gadgets has both positive and negative impact on their development. It depends on the time children spent with gadgets and the content they watch. Young children can operate touch screens with ease and modern gadgets have lot of features and applications to keep children entertained. Technology is definitely a boon for children if they explore educational apps, videos and programmes for limited time. When children watch such programmes, they acquire knowledge, learn new things and improve their vocabulary.

On the contrary, gadgets are harmful for young children if they use for longer hours. It might cause both physical and mental health issues like visual problems, obesity, sleeping disorders, attention problems etc. Apart from this, as internet is widely accessible to today's generation, children can explore unwanted content like porn videos, violent programmes etc.

Hence it is extremely important for parents to regulate children usage time and monitor the content. Parents need to be aware of experts' recommendations on children screen time and educate their children. Parental co-viewing and interaction with them while watching the programs are helpful for children to understand the concepts and associate with real life situations. To divert children from screen time, parents can engage them with a variety of indoor and outdoor activities like games, sports, puzzles, mazes, building blocks, art and craft activities, stories, book reading etc which are helpful for their holistic development.

Schools play a remarkable influence on students' and their parents' thinking. So schools need to organize parent awareness programmes and educate children on gadget usage. Teachers can provide interesting and innovative home assignments for children so that children's time can be utilized productively and keep them away from gadgets.

Experts in the field of child development like early childhood policy makers, pediatricians, counselors and academicians need to spread the awareness among parents on safety measures of gadget usage by young children. Through parent orientation programmes, blogs, websites, news letters and apps experts can reach parents and educate them on child friendly apps, password protection and child safe modes and effective ways to engage children.

Limitations of the Study:

- The present study is limited to a sample of 200 children, 200 mothers and 60 preschool teachers who were selected from private preschools of Hyderabad. Hence the findings are confined to urban population.
- Out of five tools, findings from four tools are based on the expressed opinions of the respondents so the objectivity is limited to the honesty of the subjects.
- The data is confined to 6 electronic gadgets – television, smartphone, computer, laptop, tablet/IPad and game console.
- In the present study, the influence of the usage of electronic gadgets is limited to two developmental areas i.e. language and social domains of preschool children.

IMPLICATIONS OF THE STUDY

For Parents:

- Parents should have knowledge on recommended screen time for their children and child safety measures on gadget usage.
- Parents have to regulate their children gadget usage time and monitor them.
- Parents need to spend quality time with their children by involving themselves in indoor and outdoor activities.
- Parents can take advice from child experts like pediatricians, counselors and educationists at regular intervals and seek clarifications on gadget usage.

For Schools:

- Schools need to upgrade their knowledge on latest recommendations of professionals and educate parents and students.
- Schools can organize parent education programs periodically and spread awareness on advantages and disadvantages of gadget usage and child safety precautions.
- Schools can also share the information to parents through parent portals and monthly news letters.

- ❖ Schools should allocate students with home assignments wherein they borrow books from the library and make use of their time efficiently at home instead of hanging around with gadgets.
- ❖ Teachers can educate parents during PTMs on how to engage children with various indoor activities at home.

For Government and NGOs:

- ❖ Government and NGOs can strengthen the parents counseling centers to impart parent education programmes.

Suggestions for Future Research:

- ❖ The present study includes children with preschool age group (3 to 6 years). This study can also be done on different age groups – toddlers, secondary school children, high school children, adolescents, adults and old age people.
- ❖ It is recommended that the present study can be repeated as a comparative study with rural sample.
- ❖ The present is confined to 6 electronic gadgets – television, smartphone, computer, laptop, tablet/IPad and game console. Other gadgets can be included for future research.
- ❖ It is recommended to study the influence of electronic gadgets on different domains other than language and social skills like motor skills, cognitive development, emotional development, creativity, attention problem, anxiety, sleeping disorder, eating disorder and other health issues.
- ❖ A separate study can be done by taking any one particular electronic gadget and its influence on various developments.
- ❖ The present study involves mothers' and teachers' perceptions towards children usage of electronic gadgets. In the same way, fathers, other family members and child professionals like academicians, counselors, pediatricians etc perceptions can also be studied.

References

AAP Council on Communications and Media. 2016. Media and Young Minds. *Journal of Pediatrics*. 138 (5). Retrieved 10th Jan 2019 from https://pediatrics.aappublications.org/content/138/5/e20162591

Abreu, C.N. (Eds.). 2011. Internet Addiction: A Handbook and Guide to Evaluation and Treatment. John Wiley & Sons.

Achenbach, T.M. 1991. Manual for the Child Behavior Checklist/4- 18 and 1991 Profile. Burlington, VT: University of Vermont, Department of Psychiatry.

Adamiak, L. 2015. Exploratory Study of Parent's Perceptions of Their Preschooler's Screen Media Usage. Spring 5-2015. University of San Diego. Retrieved 11th Dec 2018 from https://digital.sandiego.edu/cgi/viewcontent.cgi?article=1007&context=honors_theses

Almeida, A.N.D., Delicado, A., Alves, N.D.A., Carvalho, T. 2015. Internet, Children and Space: Revisiting Generational Attributes and Boundaries. *Journal of New Media and Society*, 17(9), 14361453. doi:10.1177/1461444814528293

American Academy of Pediatrics. 2009. Policy Statement – Media Violence. *Journal of American Academy of Pediatrics*. 124 (5). 1495-1503. https://pediatrics.aappublications.org/content/pediatrics/124/5/1495.full.pdf

Anderson, D.R., Huston, A.C., Schmitt, K.L., Linebarger, D.L., Wright, J.C. 2001. Early Childhood Television viewing and Adolescent Behavior: The Recontact Study. *Journal of Monographs of the Society for Research in Child Development*, 66(1), 1-147.

Anderson, D.R., Pempek, T.A. 2005. "Television and Very Young Children". Computers in a Developmentally Appropriate Curriculum. Young Children. 55 (2), 90-93.

Anderson, S.E., Economos, C.D., Must, A. 2008. Active Play and Screen Time in us Children Aged 4 to 11 years in Relation to Socio-demographic and Weight Status Characteristics: A Nationally Representative Cross-sectional Analysis. *Journal of BMC Public Health*. 8(1), 366.

Anderson, C.A., Shibuya, A., Ihori, N., Swing, E.L., Bushman, B.J., Sakamoto, A., Rothstein H.R., Saleem, M. 2010. Violent Video Game Effects on Aggression, Empathy, and Pro-social Behavior in Eastern and Western Countries: A Meta-analytic Review. *Journal of Psychological Bulletin*. 136(2), 151-173.

Bandura, 1973. Aggression: A Social Learning Theory Analysis, Prentice Hall, Englewood Cliffs, NJ, USA.

Bandura, A. 1977. Social Learning Theory. New York: General Learning Press.

Bansal S., Mahajan R.C. 2017. Impact of Mobile use amongst Children in Rural Area of Marathwada Region of Maharashtra, India. *International Journal of Contemporary Pediatrics*. 5(1), 50-54.

Barr, R. 2010. Transfer of Learning between 2D and 3D Sources during Infancy: Informing Theory and Practice. *Journal of Developmental Review*. 30(2), 128-54.

Barr, R., Lerner, C. 2014. Screen Sense: Setting the record Straight. Research-based Guidelines for Screen use for Children under 3 Years Old. Zero to Three. Retrieved 14th Apr 2017 from https://nyspep.org/application/files/4015/0005/1044/Screen_Sense_-_White_Paper.pdf

Barr, R., Wyss, N. 2008. Reenactment of Televised content by 2-year Olds: Toddlers use Language Learned from Television to Solve a Difficult Imitation Problem. *Journal of Infant Behavior & Development*, 31(4), 696-703. http://dx.doi.org/10.1016/j.infbeh.2008.04.006

Barr-Anderson, D.J., Jayne, A., Fulkerson, Smyth, M., Himes, J.H., Hannan, P.J., MStat, Rock, B.H., Story, M. 2011. Associations of American Indian Children's Screen-Time Behavior With Parental Television Behavior, Parental Perceptions of Children's Screen Time, and Media-Related Resources in the Home. *Journal Preventing Chronic Disease – Public Health Research*, Practice and Policy. 8, (5), A105. www.cdc.gov/pcd/issues/2011/sep/10_0241.htm

Barron, B., Cayton-Hodges, G., Bofferding, L., Copple, C., Hammond, L.D., Levine, M.H. 2011. Take a Giant Step: A Blueprint for Teaching Young Children in a Digital Age. New York: Joan Ganz Cooney Center at Sesame Workshop. Retrieved 24th May 2018 from http://www.joanganzcooneycenter.org/wp-content/uploads/2012/01/jgcc_takeagiantstep1.pdf

Bawden, D. 2008. Origins and Concepts of Digital Literacy. In C. Lankshear, M. Knobel (Eds.), *Digital Literacies: Journal of Concepts, Policies and Practices*.17-32. New York, NY: Peter Lang Publishing.

Beauchamp, M.H., Anderson, V. 2010. SOCIAL: An Integrative Framework for the Development of Social Skills. *Journal of Psychological Bulletin*, 136(1), 39-64. doi:10.1037/a0017768

Behrens, P., Rathgeb, T. 2012. FIM 2011: Familie, Interaktion & Medien: Untersuchung zur Kommunikation und Mediennutzung in Familien Retrieved 22nd Feb 2018 from http://www.mpfs.de/fileadmin/FIM/FIM2011.pdf

Bhatia, Goyal, A. 2018. Anxiety Disorders in Children and Adolescents: Need for Early Detection. *Journal of Postgraduate Medicine*. 64 (2), 75-76. doi: 10.4103/jpgm.JPGM_65_18

Bhattacharyya. 2015. Addiction to Modern Gadgets and Technologies Across Generations India. *Eastern Journal of Psychiatry*. 18 (2), 27-37.

Bickham, D.S., Rich, M. 2006. Is Television Viewing Associated with Social Isolation? Roles of Exposure Time, Viewing Context, and Violent content. *Journal of Pediatrics and Adolescent Medicine*. 160(4), 387-92.

Bilance, 1997. "A World in Balance – Bilance Stands for Social Development: Policy Paper". Oegstgeest. Retrieved 5th Sep. 2018 from http://dotcue.net/swtn/upload_newfiles/2.SocialDevelopment-TheConcept.pdf

Bittman, M., Rutherford, L., Brown, J. 2011. Digital natives? New and Old Media and Children's Outcomes. *Australian Journal of Education*. 55(2), 161-175. http://dx.doi.org/10.1177/000494411105500206

Blackwell, C.K., Lauricella, A.R., Wartella, E. 2014. Factors Influencing Digital Technology use in Early Childhood Education. *Journal of Computers & Education*. 77, 82-90.

Blankson, A.N., O'Brien, M., Leerkes, E.M., Calkins, S.D., Marcovitch, S. 2015. Do Hours Spent viewing Television at Ages 3 and 4 Predict Vocabulary and Executive Functioning at Age 5? *Journal of Merrill-Palmer Quarterly*, 61(2), 264-289. doi:10.13110/merrpalmquar1982.61.2.0264

Bornstein, M., Hahn, C.S, Haynes, O. 2004. Specific and General Language Performance Across Early Childhood: Stability and Gender Considerations. *Journal of First Language*, 24(3), 267-304.

Bovill, M., Livingstone, S.M. 2001. "Bedroom Culture and the Privatisation of Media Use". London: LSE Research Online. Retrieved 21st May 2018 from http://eprints.lse.ac.uk/672/1/Chapter8_ Children% 26 Changing MediaEnvironment.pdf.

Bowlby J. 1980. Attachment and Loss. Volume 3. Loss, Sadness and Depression. New York: Basic Books.

Boynton-Jarrett, R., Thomas, T.N., Peterson, K.E., Wiecha. J., Sobol, A.M., Gortmaker, S.L. 2003. Impact of Television viewing Patterns on Fruit and Vegetable Consumption among Adolescents. *Journal of Pediatrics*. 112, 1321-1326.

Brouwer, C., Duimel, M., Jansen, S., Nikken, P., Pardoen, J., & Pijpers, R. 2011. App Noot Muis. Peuters en kleuters op het internet: Buurtboek: Leiden. Retrieved 22nd Feb. 2013 from https://ibimapublishing.com/articles/JMTKS/2016/109393/109393.pdf

Bukato, D., 2008. Child and Adolescent Development, A Chronological Approach, Houghton Mifflin Company, Boston.

Burdette, Hillary, L., Robert, C., Whitaker. 2005. Resurrecting Free Play in Young Children: Looking Beyond Fitness and Fatness to Attention, Affiliation, and Affect. *Journal of Pediatrics and Adolescent Medicine.* 159 (1), 46-50.

Burstein, M., Ginsburg, G.S., Tein, J.Y. 2010. Parental Anxiety and Child Symtomology: An Examination of Addictive and Interactive Effects of Parent Psychopathology. Journal of Abnormal Child Psychology. 38 (7), 897-909.

Calvert, S.L., Rideout, V.J., Woolard, J.L., Barr, R.F. Strouse, G.A. 2005. Age, Ethnicity, and Socioeconomic Patterns in Early Computer use: A National Survey. *Journal of American Behavioural Scientist*, 48, 590-607.

Carl, A., Dawson, Warner, E., Gettys.1948. An Introduction to Sociology. Edition 3. Ronald Press, New York.

Cavanaugh, C., Gillian, K.J., Kromrey, J., Hess, M., Blomeyer, R. 2004. The Effects of Distance Education on K–12 Student Outcomes: A Meta-analysis: Naperville, Ill.: Learning Point Associates. Retrieved 20th Dec. 2018 from https://files.eric.ed.gov/fulltext/ED489533.pdf

Chaudron, S. 2015. Young Children (0-8) and Digital Technology. A Qualitative Exploratory Study Across Seven Countries. JSR Science and Policy Reports. Retrieved 20th Aug 2018 from http://www.lse.ac.uk/media@lse/research/ToddlersAndTablets/RelevantPublications/Young-Children-(0-8)-and-Digital-Technology.pdf

Chiong, C., Shuler, C. 2010. Learning: Is there an app for that? Investigations of Young Children's Usage and Learning with Mobile Devices and Apps. New York: The Joan Ganz Cooney Center at Sesame Workshop. Retrieved from https://clalliance.org/wp-content/uploads/files/learningapps_final_110410.pdf

Chomsky, N. 1975. Reflections on Language. Pantheon Books, New York.

Christakis, D,A., Garrison, M.M, Herrenkohl, T. 2013. Modifying Media Content for Preschool Children: A Randomized Controlled Trial. *Journal of Pediatrics.* 131(3), 431-8.

Christakis, D. 2009. The Effects of Infant Media Usage: What do we know and what should we learn? *Journal of Acta Paediatrica*, 98(1), 8-16. http://dx.doi.org/10.1111/j.1651-2227.2008.01027.x

Christakis, D.A., Zimmerman, F.J., DiGiuseppe, D.L., McCarty, C.A. 2004. Early Television Exposure and Subsequent Attentional Problems in Children. *Journal of Pediatrics,* 113(4), 708-713.

Committee on Public Education. 2001. Children, Adolescents, and Television. *Journal of Pediatrics,* 107, 423-426.

Conners-Burrow, N.A., McKelvey, L.M., Fussell, J.J. 2011. Social outcomes associated with media viewing Habits of Low-income Preschool Children. *Journal of Early Education and Development,* 22(2), 256-273. doi: 10.1080/10409289.2011.550844

Crux Research. 2015. Parent Poll: Better Hearing and Speech Month. Retrieved from de Almeida,A.N., Delicado, A., de Almeida Alves, N., & Carvalho, T. 2015. Internet, Children and Space: Revisiting Generational Attributes and Boundaries. New Media & Society, 17 (9), 1436-1453.

Daly, L.A., Perez, L.M. 2008. Exposure to Media Violence and Other Correlates of Aggressive Behavior in Preschool Children. *Journal of Early Childhood Research and Practice.* 11 (2). Retrieved 17th July 2017 from https://www.semanticscholar.org/paper/Exposure-to-Media-Violence-and-Other-Correlates-of-Daly-P%C3%A9rez/c0650b7d82b1e8eccf7a2c3d18c7b95f942be504

David, L. 2014. "Social Development Theory (Vygotsky)" in Learning Theories. Retrieved 5th Sep 2018 from https://www.learning-theories.com/vygotskys-social-learning-theory.html

Dietz, W.H., Gortmaker, S.L. 1985. Do we Fatten our Children at the Television set? Obesity and Television viewing in Children and Adolescents. *Journal of Pediatrics.* 75, 807-812.

Disney, L., Barnes, A., McDowall, J., Geng, G. 2013. Observation of Children's Engagement when Playing iPads. In L.H. Wong, C.C. Liu, T. Hirashima, P. Sumedi, M. Lukman (Eds.), Proceedings of the 21st International Conference on Computers in Education (pp. 616-621). Indonesia: Asia-Pacific Society for Computers in Education.

Donohue, C. 2010. "There's an App for (Almost) Everything: New Technology Tools for EC Professionals—Part 2". *Journal of Exchange.* 195, 40-44. https://secure.ccie.com/library/5019540.pdf

Donovan, J.E. 2005. Problem Behavior Theory. *Journal of Encyclopedia of Applied Developmental Science.* Vol. 2, 872-877.

Downes, T. 2002. Blending Play, Practice and Performance: Children's use of the Computer at Home. *The Journal of Educational Enquiry,* 3(2), 21-34.

Downey, D.B., Condron, D.J. 2004. Playing well with others in Kindergarten: The Benefits of Siblings at Home. *Journal of Marriage and Family,* 66, 333-350.

Downey, S., Hayes, N., O'Neill, B. 2007. Play and Technology for Children Aged 4-12. Centre for Social and Educational Research, Dublin Institute of Technology. Retrieved 14th Apr 2018 from https://arrow.dit.ie/cgi/viewcontent.cgi?referer=https://www.google.com/&httpsredir=1&article=1000&context=cserrep

Drago, E. 2015. The Effect of Technology on Face-to-Face Communication. The Elon Journal of Undergraduate Research in Communications, *Spring Journal*. 6 (1), 13-19. https://www.elon.edu/docs/e-web/academics/communications/research/vol6no1/02DragoEJSpring15.pdf

Duch, H., Fisher, E.M., Ensari, I., Font, M., Harrington, A., Taromino, C., Rodriguez, C. 2013. Association of Screen Time use and Language Development in Hispanic Toddlers: A Cross-sectional and Longitudinal Study. *Journal of Clinical Pediatrics*, 52 (9), 857-865. doi:10.1177/0009922813492881

Edmunds, K.M., Bauserman, K.L. 2006. What Teachers can Learn about Reading Motivation through Conversations with Children. *Journal of Reading Teacher.* 59, 414-424.

Erikson Institute Report. 2016. Technology and young Children in the Digital Age. Retrieved 20th Aug 2018 from https://www.erikson.edu/wp-content/uploads/2018/07/Erikson-Institute-Technology-and-Young-Children-Survey.pdf

Fergusson, D.M. 2005. Horwood LJ, Ridder EM. Show me the Child at Seven: The Consequences of Conduct Problems in Childhood for Psychosocial Functioning in Adulthood. J Child Psychol. *Journal of Psychiatry*. 46(8), 837-49.

Fish, A.M., MC Carrick, K., Stanton, B., Brunitt, G.A., Partridge, T. 2008. Early Childhood Computer Experience and Cognitive Development among Urban Low Income Preschoolers. *Journal of Educational Computing Research.* 38(1), 97-113. Doi: 10.2190/EC.38.1.e

Fivush, R., Brotman, M.A., Buckner, J.P., Goodman, S.H. 2000. Gender differences in Parent-child Emotion Narratives. *Journal of Sex Roles*. 42 (3-4), 233-253. https://doi.org/10.1023/A:1007091207068

Fletcher, E.N., Whitaker, R.C., Marino, A.J., Anderson, S.E. 2014. Screen Time at Home and School among Low-income Children Attending Head Start. *Journal of Child Indicators Research.* 7(2), 421-436. http://doi.org/10.1007/s12187-013-9212-8.

Friederici, A.D. 2011. The Brain basis of Language Processing: from Structure to Function. *Journal of Physiological Reviews.* 91 (4), 1357-92. doi: 10.1152/physrev.00006.2011.

Friefrich, K.L. Stein, H.A. 2007. Aggression and Pro-social Television Programmes and the Natural Bahaviour of Pre-school Children: Thousand Oaks: Sage publications.

Fussell, J.J., Conners-Burrow, N.A., McKelvey, L.M. 2011. Social outcomes associated with Media viewing Habits of Low-income Preschool Children. *Journal of Early Education and Development.* 22(2), 256-273. doi: 10.1080/10409289.2011.550844

Gachuru, F.W. 2012. Effects of Television Programming on Preschool Children's Social Development in Westlands District, Nairobi. University of Nairobi. Retrieved 17th Jan 2019 from https://pdfs.semanticscholar.org/f3b0/436337b44dcb59c144c2b452d9fcdad55916.pdf

Gani, S.A. 2016. Parenting Digital Natives/: Cognitive, Emotional, and Social Developmental Challenges. *International Conference on Education,* 870-880. Retrieved 17th Jan 2019 from file:///C:/Users/srmanchala/Downloads/118-229-2-PB.pdf

Ghavifekr, S., Rosdy, W.A.W. 2015. Teaching and Learning with Technology: Effectiveness of ICT Integration in Schools. *International Journal of Research in Education and Science.* 1(2), 175-191.

Gibbons. P. 2009. English Learners, Academic Literacy and Thinking. Retrieved 15th May 2018 from http://www.collaborativelearning.org/academiclitchap1.pdf

Given, L.M., Winkler, D.C., Willson, R., Davidson, C., Danby, S., Torpe, K. 2014. Documenting Young Children's Technology Use: Observations in the Home. Retrieved 5th Nov 2014 from https://onlinelibrary.wiley.com/doi/10.1002/meet.2014.14505101028

Goh, W., Bay, S., Chen, V. 2015. Young School Children's use of Digital Devices and Parental Rules. *Telematics and Informatics,* 32(4), 787-795. doi:10.1016/j.tele.2015.04.002

Grabmeier, J. 2012. Preschoolers' Reading Skills Benefit from One modest change by Teachers. *Journal of Education Digest: Essential Readings Condensed for Quick Review,* 78 (1), 63-64.

Griffiths, L., Dowda, M., Dezateux, C., Pate, R.R. 2010, "Associations between Sport and Screen-entertainment with Mental Health Problems in 5-year-old Children", *International Journal of Behavioral Nutrition and Physical Activity.* 7 (30), 1-11. https:// doi.org/10.1186/1479-5868-7-30.

Guernsey, L. 2012. Screen Time: How Electronic Media—from Baby Videos to Educational Software—Affects your Young Child. New York, NY: Basic Books.

Guomundsdottir, G.B., Hardersen, B. 2011. Toddlers Digital Universe: 0-6-year-olds Access to and use of Digital Devices in your Spare Time Retrieved 21st Feb. 2018, from https://iktsenteret.no/ressurser/smabarns-digitale-univers

Hanna, L.E. 2016. Parent Perceptions of Technology on Children's Language Development. *Spring Journal.* Retrieved 11th Apr 2019 from https://scholars.unh.edu/cgi/viewcontent.cgi?referer=https://www.google.com/&httpsredir=1&article=1300&context=honors

Hastings, E.C., Karas, T.L., Winsler, A., Way, E., Madigan, A., Tyler, S. 2009. Young Children's Video/Computer Game use: Relations with School Performance and Behavior. *Journal of Issues in Mental Health Nursing, 30, 638-649.*

Hatzigianni, M., Margetts, K. 2014. Parents' Beliefs and Evaluations of Young Children's Computer use. *Australasian Journal of Early Childhood.* 39(4), 114-122.

Heim, J., Brandtzaeg, P.B., Karre, B.H., Endestad, T., Torgersen, L. 2007. Children's Usage of Media Technologies and Psychosocial Factors. *Journal of New Media and Society,* 9(3), 425-454.

Hill, A. 2015. Exclusive Survey: Parents Weigh in on the Digital Classroom. Retrieved 22nd May 2017, from https://www.marketplace.org/2015/05/15/exclusive-survey-parents-weigh-digital-classroom/

Hinkley, T., Brown, H., Carson, V., Teychenne, M. 2018. Cross Sectional Associations of Screen Time and Outdoor Play with Social Skills in Preschool Children. *Journal of PLoS One.* 13(4): e0193700. https://doi.org/10.1371/journal.pone.0193700

Honig, A.S. 2007. Oral Language Development. *Journal of Early Child Development and Care,* 177(6&7), 581-613.

Hosokawa, R., Katsura, T. 2018. Association between Mobile Technology use and Child Adjustment in Early Elementary School Age. *Journal of PLoS One.* 13 (7), e0199959. https://doi.org/ 10.1371/journal.pone.0199959

International Telecommunication Union Report. 2015. ICT Facts and Figures. Retrieved 17th July 2017 from https://www.itu.int/en/ITU-D/Statistics/Documents/facts/ICTFactsFigures2015.pdf

Jessor, R., Jessor, L.S. 1977. Problem Behaviour and Psychosocial Development: A Longitudinal Study of Youth. Academy Press, New York.

Judge, S., Puckett, K., Bell, S.M. 2006. Closing the Digital Divide: Update from the Early Childhood Longitudinal Study. *Journal of Educational Research.* 100(1), 52-60. doi: 10.3200/joer.100.1.52-60.

Kaiser Family Foundation Study. 2006. The Media Family: Electronic Media in the Lives of Infants, Toddlers, Preschoolers and their Parents. Retrieved 17th Jan 2018 from https://www.kff.org/other/the-media-family-electronic-media-in-the/

Kaiser Family Foundation Study. 2010. Generation M2 – Media in the Lives of 8-18 year Olds. Retrieved 29th Aug 2018 from http://kaiserfamilyfoundation.files.wordpress.com/2013/01/8010.pdf.

Kara, N., Cagiltay, K. 2017. In-service Preschool Teachers' Thoughts about Technology and Technology Use in Early Educational Settings. *Journal of Contemporary Educational Technology.* 8(2), 119-141.

Kegan, R. 1982. The Evolving Self: Problem and Process in Human Development. Cambridge, MA: Harvard University Press.

Kirkorian, H.L., Pempek, T.A., Murphy, L.A., Schmidt, M.E., Anderson, D.R. 2009. The Impact of Background Television on Parent-child Interaction. *Journal of Child Development,* 80, 1350-1359.

Klarin, M. 2016. Conceptual Challenges in Understanding Innovative Education in Organizational Context. *International Journal of Cognitive Research in Science, Engineering and Education.* 4(1), 67-71.

Koskinen, P.S., Blum, I.H., Bisson, S.A., Phillips, S.M., Creamer, T.S., Baker, T.K. 2000. Book Access, Shared Reading, and Audio Models: The Effects of Supporting the Literacy Learning of Linguistically Diverse Students in School and at Home. *Journal of Educational Psychology.* 92(1), 23-36.

Krcmar, M., Grela, B.G., Lin, Y. 2007. Can Toddlers Learn Vocabulary from Television? An Experimental Approach. *Journal of Media Psychology,* 10, 41-63.

Kuhl, P.K. 2004. Early Language Acquisition: Cracking the Speech Code. *Journal of Nature Reviews Neuroscience.* 5, 831-843.

Kutner, L., Olson, C. 2008. Grand Theft Childhood: The Surprising Truth about Violent Video Games and what Parents can do. New York, NY: Simon and Schuster. https://psycnet.apa.org/record/2008-03242-000

Landhuis, C.E., Poulton, R., Welch, D., Hancox, R.J. 2007. Does Childhood Television viewing Lead to Attention Problems in Adolescence? Results from a Prospective Longitudinal Study. *Journal of Pediatrics,* 120, 532-537.

Lanigan, J.D., Bold, M., Chenoweth, L. 2009. Computers in the Family Context: Perceived Impact on Family Time and Relationships. *Family Science Review,* 14 (1), 16-32.

Lemetyinen, H. 2012. Language Acquisition. Simply Psychology. Retrieved 29th Aug 2018 from https://www.simplypsychology.org/language.html

Lillard, A.S., Peterson, J. 2011. The Immediate Impact of Different Types of Television on Young Children's Executive Function. *Journal of Pediatrics.* 128 (4), 644-649.

Lin, L.Y., Cherng, R.J., Chen, Y.J., Yang, H.M. 2015. Effects of Television Exposure on Developmental Skills Among Young Children. *Journal of Infant Behaviour Development.* 38: 20-6.

Lindita, S. Fauzi S. 2017. Teachers' Perceptions of Technology use in the Classroom. University of Tetovo – Tetovo, Republic of Macedonia. Retrieved 2nd Feb. 2019 from https://www.researchgate.net/publication/328492337_ TEACHERS'_ PERCEPTIONS_ OF_ TECHNOLOGY_ USE_IN_THE_CLASSROOM

Linebarger, D. L., Walker, D. 2005. Infants' and Toddlers' Television Viewing and Language outcomes. *Journal of American Behavioral Scientist.* 48(5), 624-645. http://dx.doi.org/10.1177/0002764204271505

Linebarger, D.L., Piotrowski, J. 2009. TV as Storyteller: How Exposure to Television Narratives Impacts at-risk Preschoolers' Story Knowledge and Narrative Skills. British *Journal of Developmental Psychology,* 27(1), 47-69. http://dx.doi.org/10.1348/026151008X400445

Linebarger, D.L., Vaala, S. E. 2010. Screen Media and Language Development in Infants and Toddlers: An Ecological Perspective. Developmental Review, 30(2), 176-202. http://dx.doi.org/10.1016/j.dr.2010.03.006

Ling, R., Yttri, B. 2006. Control, Emancipation, and Status: The Mobile Telephone in Teens' Parental and Peer Relationships. In R. Kraut, M. Brynin, & S. Kiesler (Eds.), Computers, Phones, and the Internet: Domesticating Information Technology. New York, NY: Oxford University Press. 219-234.

Magnauson, K.A, Sexton, H.R., Davis-Kean, P.E., Huston, A.C. 2009. Increases in Maternal Education and Language Skills. *Journal of Merrill-Palmer Quarterly,* 55 (3), 319-350. https://www.jstor.org/stable/23096260?seq=1#page_scan_tab_contents

Mainiero, L.A., Sullivan, S.E. 2005. Kaleidoscope Careers: An Alternate Explanation for the "opt-out Revolution. *Journal of Academy of Management Executive,* 19(1), 106-123.

Manivannan, D., Srinivasa, G., Francis, R.M. 2017. A Study to Assess the Knowledge Regarding Behavioral Problems of School Children among Mothers. *IOSR Journal of Nursing and Health Science.* 6 (6), 13-16.

Marianne K. 2015. Young Children as Internet Users and Parents Perspectives. University of Oulu, Retrieved 12th Dec 2018 from http://jultika.oulu.fi/files/nbnfioulu-201505261650.pdf

McClelland, M.M., Morrison, F.J., Holmes, D.L. 2000. Children at Risk for Early Academic Problems: The Role of Learning-related Social Skills. *Journal of Early Childhood Research Quarterly, 15*(3), 307-329. doi:10.1016/S0885-2006(00)00069-7

McCloskey, M., Johnson, S.L., Benz, C., Thompson, D.A., Chamberlin, B., Clark, L., Bellows, L.L. 2017. Parent Perceptions of Mobile Device Use among Preschool-Aged Children in Rural Head Start Centers, *Journal of Nutrition Education and Behavior.* 50 (1), 83-89.

Mendelsohn, A.L., Brockmeyer, C.A., Dreyer, B.P., Fierman, A.H., Berkule-Silberman, S.B., Tomopoulos, S. 2010. Do Verbal Interactions with Infants during Electronic Media Exposure Mitigate Adverse Impacts on their Language Development as Toddlers? *Journal of Infant & Child Development.* 19(6), 577-593. http://dx.doi.org/10.1002/icd.711

Merrill, F.E., Eldredge, H.W. 1961. Society and Culture. An Introduction to Sociology. Second Edition. Prentice-Hall: Englewood Cliffs Publishers.

Mol, S.E., Bus, A.G. 2011. To Read or Not to Read: A Meta-Analysis of Print Exposure From Infancy to Early Adulthood, *Journal of Psychological Bulletin,* 137, 267-296.

Monika Sharma, 2012. Addiction of Youth towards Gadgets. *Journal of Elixir Human Resource Management.* 42A, 6568-6572. Retrieved 1st May 2018 from https://www.elixirpublishers.com/articles/1350727799_42A%20(2012)%206568-6572.pdf

Morine, K.A., Crothers, L.M., Schreiber, J.B., Kolbert, J.B., Hughes, T.L., Schmitt, A.J. 2011. Relational Aggression in Preschool Students: An Exploration of the Variables of Sex, Age, and Siblings. Hindawi Publishing Corporation. *Journal of Child Development Research.* Article ID 931720. Retrieved 18th Dec 2018 from http://downloads.hindawi.com/journals/cdr/2011/931720.pdf

Morrison, M., Krugman, M. 2001. "A Look at Mass and Computer Mediated Technologies: Understanding the Roles of Television and Computers in the Home." *Journal of Broadcasting and Electronic Media.* 45(1):135-161.

NAEYC Report. 2009. "Developmentally Appropriate Practice in Early Childhood Programs Serving Children from Birth through Age 8". Position statement. Retrieved 17th Sep 2016 from www.naeyc.org/files/naeyc/file/positions/PSDAP.pdf.

NAEYC report. 2012. "Technology and Interactive Media as Tools in Early Childhood Programs Serving Children from Birth through Age 8", Fred Rogers Center for Early Learning and Children's Media at Saint Vincent College. Retrieved 6th May 2017 from https://www.naeyc.org/sites/default/files/globally-shared/downloads/PDFs/resources/topics/PS_technology_WEB.pdf

National Association for the Education of Young Children (NAEYC), Fred Rogers Center for Early Learning and Chil-dren's Media. 2012. Retrieved 10th Jan 2019 from https://www.naeyc.org/sites/default/files/globally-shared/downloads/PDFs/resources/topics/12_KeyMessages_Technology.pdf

National Institute of Mental Health (NIMH). 1982. Television and Behavior: Ten Years of Scientific Progress and Implications for the Eighties: Vol. 1. Summary Report. Washington, DC: Government Printing Office. Retrieved 10th Oct 2018 from https://files.eric.ed.gov/fulltext/ED222186.pdf

Nielsen's National Television Household Universe Estimates. 2016. Retrieved 10th Oct. 2017 from http://www.nielsen.com/us/en/about-us/nielsen-families.html

Nikken, P., de Haan, J. 2015. Guiding Young Children's Internet use at Home: Problems that Parents Experience in their Parental Mediation and the need for Parenting Support. Cyberpsychology. *Journal of Psychosocial Research on Cyberspace.* 9(1), Article 3. doi: 10.5817/CP2015-1-3

Nikken, P., Schols, M. 2015. How and Why Parents Guide the Media Use of Young Children. Springer. *Journal of Child and Family Studies.* 24: 3423-3435. DOI 10.1007/s10826-015-0144-4.

Nikolopoulou, K., Gialamas, V. 2009. Investigating Pre-service Early Childhood Teachers' Views and Intentions about Integrating and using Computers in Early Childhood Settings: Compilation of an Instrument. *Journal of Technology, Pedagogy and Education.* 18(2), 201-219.

O'Neill, B., Hayes, N., Downey, S., 2005. A Study of ICTs in Play Activities of Irish Children (4-8 and 8-12)'. Centre for Social and Educational Research, Dublin Institute of Technology. Childhoods 2005, University of Oslo. Conference Paper. Retrieved 24th May 2018 from https://arrow.dit.ie/cgi/viewcontent.cgi?referer=https://www.google.com/&httpsredir=1&article=1015&context=aaschmedcon

Ofcom Report. 2013. Children and Parents: Media use and Attitudes Report. Retrieved 07th Oct 2013 from http://stakeholders.ofcom.org.uk/binaries/research/media-literacy/october-2013/research.pdf

Ofcom Report. 2017. Children and Parents: Media Use and Attitudes Report. Retrieved 11th Dec. 2018 from https://www.ofcom.org.uk/__data/assets/pdf_file/0020/108182/children-parents-media-use-attitudes-2017.pdf

Olson, C.K., Kutner, L.A., Baer, L., Beresin, E.V., Warner, D.E., Nicholi II, A.M. 2009. M-rated Video Games and Aggressive or Problem Behavior among Young Adolescents. *Journal of Applied Developmental Science.* 13(4), 188-198.

Owens, J., Maxim, R., McGuinn, M., Nobile, C., Msall, M., Alario, A. 1999. Television-viewing Habits and Sleep Disturbance in School Children. *Journal of Pediatrics.* Vol. 104. Retrieved 4th Apr 2019 from https://www.ncbi.nlm.nih.gov/pubmed/10469810

Paavonen, E.J., Pennonen, M., Roine, M., Valkonen, S., Lahikainen, A.R. 2006. TV Exposure Associated with Sleep Disturbances in 5-to 6-year-old Children. *Journal of Sleep Research.* 15, 154-161.

Parent, J., Sanders, W., Forehand, R. 2016. Youth Screen Time and Behavioral Health Problems: The Role of Sleep duration and Disturbances. *Journal of Developmental and Behavioural Pediatrics.* 37 (4), 277-284. doi: 10.1097/DBP.0000000000000272.

Pasqua. S., Mancini, A.L. 2012. Asymmetries and Interdependencies in Time Use Between Italian Parents. *Journal of Applied Economics*, 44(32), 4153-4171.

Patterson, G.R., Fisher, P.A. 2002. Recent Developments in our understanding of Parenting: Bidirectional Effects, Causal Models, and the Search for Parsimony. *Handbook of Parenting*. 5, 59-88.

Patrick, N.J. 2008. Social Skills for Teenagers and Adults with Sperger Syndrome: London and Philadelphia: Jessica Kingsley Publishers.

Pearson's National Literacy Trust. 2014. Practitioner Perspectives: Children's Use of Technology in the Early Years. (Online report) Retrieved 24th May 2018 https://files.eric.ed.gov/fulltext/ED560655.pdf

Penjuree, K., Penjira, K. 2012. Perception of Primary School Students, Parents and Teachers toward the Use of Computers, the Internet and Social Networking sites. *Journal of Procedia Social and Behavioral Sciences*. 88, 282-290.

Pew Research Center Report. 2016. Technology Device Ownership: 2015. Retrieved 10th Oct 2018. from https://www.pewinternet.org/2015/10/29/technology-device-ownership-2015/

Plowman, L., McPake, J., Stephen, C. 2010. "The Technologisation of Childhood? Young Children and Technology in the Home." *Journal of Children & Society*. 24(1), 63-74.

Priyadarshini, R., Sundar, J.S., Valarmathi, S., Kalpana, S., Srijayanth, P. 2013. Impact of Media on the Physical Health of Urban School Children of Age Group 11-17 yrs. in Chennai - A Cross Sectional Study. *IOSR Journal of Humanities and Social Science (IOSR-JHSS)*. 9 (5), 30-35.

Pruksananonda, C., Chonchaiya, W., 2008. Television Viewing Associates with Delayed Language Development. *Journal of Acta Paediatrica*, 97, 977-982.

Radesky, J., Miller, A.L., Rosenblum, K.L., Appugliese, D., Kaciroti, N., Lumeng, J.C. 2015. Maternal Mobile Device use during a Structured Parent-child Interaction Task. *Journal of Academic Pediatrics*. 15 (2), 238-244.

Rai, S., Malik, S.C., Sharma, D. 1993. Behavior Problems among Preschool Children. *Journal of Indian Pediatrics*. 30 (4), 475-8.

Ralston, S.J. 2015. What's Wrong with Distracted Parenting? An Ethical Analyses. Retrieved 12th June 2019 from https://www.academia.edu/19842806/Whats_ Wrong_ with_ Distracted_ Parenting_ An_ Ethical_Analysis

Ray, C.E., Elliott, S.N. 2006. Social Adjustment and Academic Achievement: A Predictive Model for Students with Diverse Academic and Behavior Competencies. *Journal of School Psychology Review*, 35(3), 493-501.

Ray, M., Kana, R.J., 2010. Effect of Electronic Media on Children, *Journal of Indian Paediatrics*. Vol. 47, 561-568.

Rhodes, A. 2017. Screen Time and Kids: What's happening in our Homes? Australian Child Health Pole Report. Retrieved 19th Nov 2018 from https://www.rchpoll.org.au/wp-content/uploads/2017/06/ACHP-Poll7_Detailed-Report-June21.pdf.

Ribner, A., Fitzpatrick. C., Blair, C. 2017. Family Socioeconomic status Moderates Associations between Television Viewing and School Readiness Skills. *Journal of Developmental and Behavioural Pediatrics*. 38(3), 233-9.

Rideout, V.J. 2004. The Role of Media in Childhood Obesity. Proceedings of the Senate Committee on Commerce, Science & Transportation Subcommittee on Competition, Foreign Commerce, and Infrastructure, Retrieved 8th Nov 2017 from http://www.kff.org/kaiserpolls/loader.cfm?url==/commonspot/security/getfile.cfm&Page

Rideout, V.J., Hamel, E. 2006. The Media Family: Electronic Media in the Lives of Infants, Toddlers, Preschoolers and their Parents. Menlo Park, CA: Kaiser Family Foundation.

Rideout, V.J., Vandewater, Elizabeth, A., Wartella, Ellen, A. 2003. Zero to Six. Electronic Media in the Lives of Infants, Toddlers and Preschoolers. Fall 2003. A Kaiser Family Foundation report. Retrieved 10th Oct 2018 from https://www.scholars.northwestern.edu/en/publications/zero-to-six-electronic-media-in-the-lives-of-infants-toddlers-and

Roseberry, S., Hirsh-Pasek, K., Golinkoff, R. 2009. Live action: Can Young Children Learn Verb from Video? *Journal of Child Development*, 80(5), 1360-1375. http://dx.doi.org/10.1111/j.1467-8624.2009.01338.x

Rudd, L.C., Kelley, H.M. 2011. Encyclopedia of Child Behaviour and Development. Ed: Goldstein, S., Naglieri, J.A. Texas Tech University, Lubbock, USA.

Santa Clara County Office of Education (2016). Children and Screen Time. A Summary from the Santa Clara County Office of Education. Published by Office of Superintendent. Retrieved 2nd Feb 2019 from https://www.sccoe.org/resources/families/Documents/SCCOE-Report-English.pdf

Schepper, R. 2011. "Introducing Let's Move! Child Care: Tools for Child and Day Care Centers and Family-Care Homes." Let's Move (blog), Retrieved 24th May 2018 from www.letsmove.gov/blog/2011/06/08/introducing-let%E2%80%99smove-child-care-tools-child-and-day-care-centers-and-family-care-h

Schoon, I., Parsons, S., Rush, R., Law, J. 2010. Children's Language Ability and Psycholosocial Development: A 29-year follow-up Study. *Journal of Pediatrics*, 126(1), e73-e80.

Setliff, A.E. 2009. Debating the Impact of Television and Video Material on very Young Children: Attention, Learning, and the Developing Brain. *Journal of Child Development Perspectives*, 3(1), 72-78.

Sigman, A. 2012. The Impact of Screen Media on Children: A Eurovision for Parliament. This Chapter is based on a Verbal Presentation given to the Quality of Childhood Group in the European Parliament. Retrieved 24th May 2018 from https://www.steinereducation.edu.au/wp-content/uploads/uk_screen_time.pdf

Sinek, S., Sparkman, A. 2013. *Scholastic Kids & Family Reading Report.* New York, NY: Scholastic. Retrieved 3rd Aug 2016 from https://www.scholastic.com/readingreport/home.html

Singer, D.G., Singer, J.L. 1980. Television Viewing and Aggressive Behavior in Preschool Children: A Field Study. *Annals of the New York Academy of Sciences*, 347, 289-303.

Singh, A., Gaurav, S., 2012. Television Exposure and Academic Skills of Children: New Findings from India. *Journal of Communication Technology and Human Behaviours.* 1: 1-24. doi:10.7726/jcthb.2013.1001

Sonja, P., Milena, V.Z., Jana, K., Cirila, P. 2009. Students' Social Behaviour in Relation to their Academic Achievement in Primary and Secondary School: Teacher's Perspective. *Journal of PSIHOLOGIJSKE TEME.* 18 (1), 55-74. Retrieved 17th Jan 2018 fromhttps://pdfs.semanticscholar.org/dda9/9d4ac 22d355f07283827 c3d1c3 e419b2f58f.pdf

Stettler, N., Signer, T.M., Suter, P.M. 2001. Electronic Games and Environmental Factors Associated with Childhood Obesity in Switzerland. Journal of Obesity Research, 12, 896-903.

Stewart, S.L., Rubin, K.H. 1995. The Social Problem Solving Skills of Anxious-withdrawn Children. *Journal of Development and Psychopathology.* 7, 323-36.

Stiglic, N., Viner, R.M. 2019. The Effects of Screen Time on the Health and wellbeing of Children and Adolescents: A Systematic Review of Reviews. *BMJ Open Journal.* Vol. 9 (1). Retrieved 20th June 2019 from https://bmjopen.bmj.com/content/9/1/e023191

Straker, L.M., Mathiassen, S.E. 2009. Increased Physical Loads in Modern Work – a necessity for better Health and Performance? *Journal of Ergonomics,* 52 (10), 1215-1225.

Strouse, G.A., Troseth, G.L. 2014. Supporting Toddlers' Transfer of Word Learning from Video. *Journal of Cognitive Development.* 30, 47-64.

Subrahmanyam, K., Robert, E.K., Patricia, M.G., Elisheva, F.G. 2000. The Impact of Home Computer use on Children Activities and Development. *Journal of the Future of Children.* 10 (2), 123-144.

Swedish Media Council report, 2015. Statens Mediaråd (ed.) Småungar and Medier 2015, retrieved 10th Oct 2017 from http://www. statensmedierad.se/download/18.7a953dba14fef1148cf3a0e/14428412730 52/Sma-ungar-och-medier-2015.pdf

Swing, E.L., Gentile, D.A., Anderson, C.A. 2010. Television and Video Game Exposure and the Development of Attention Problems. *Journal of Pediatrics*. 126, 213-221.

Taylor, J. 2012. Raising Generation Tech: Prepare your Children for a Media-fueled World. Sourcebook.

Thiruchelvam, N. 2014. Attitudes towards Tablet Devices as an Educational Tool. Heriot Watt University. Retrieved 11th Dec 2018 from http://www.macs.hw.ac.uk/cs/projectsystem/projectdata/archive/2014/ugcse/nt78_full_text.pdf

Thompson, D.A., Christakis, D.A. 2005 The Association Between Television Viewing and Irregular Sleep Schedules among Children less than 3 Years of Age. *Journal of Pediatrics*. 116(4), 851-6.

Tran, P., Subrahmanyam, K. 2013. Evidence-based Guidelines for the Informal use of Computers by Children to Promote the Development of Academic, Cognitive and Social Skills, *Journal of Ergonomics*, 56 (9), 1349-1362, DOI: 10.1080/00140139.2013.820843.

Turow, J. 1999. The Internet and the Family: The View from the Parents, the view from Kids. University of Pennsylvania. Retrieved 14th Apr 2018 from https://repository.upenn.edu/cgi/viewcontent.cgi?article=1409&context=asc_papers

Umek, M.L., Peklaj, F.U. 2017. Early Vocabulary, Parental Education and the Frequency of Shared Reading as Predictors of Toddler's Vocabulary and Grammer at Age 2-7. A Slovenian longitudinal CDI study. *Journal of Child Language*. 44, 457-479.

Unicef Report. 2017. The State of the World's Children 2017, Children in a Digital World. Retrieved 12th June 2019 from https://www.unicef.org/publications/files/SOWC_2017_ENG_WEB.pdf

Vandewater, E.A., Bickham, D. S. 2004. The Impact of Educational Television on Young Children in the Context of Family Stress. *Journal of Applied Developmental Psychology*. 25, 717-728.

Vandewater, E.A., Bickham, D.S, Lee, J.H. 2006. Time well spent? Relating Television use to Children's Free-time Activities. *Journal of Pediatrics*. 117: 181-191.

Vandewater, E.A., Rideout, V.J., Wartella, E.A., Huang, X., Lee, J.H., Shim, M. 2007. Digital Childhood: Electronic Media and Technology use among Infants, Toddlers, and Preschoolers. *Journal of Pediatrics*. 119(5), 1006-1015. doi:10.1542/peds.2006-1804.

Venter, M., Wet, L.D, Swart, J. 2016. Perceptions of Parents and Teachers of the use of Mobile apps for Mathematical Education. Research Gate. Conference Paper. Retrieved 17th Jan 2019 from https://pdfs.semanticscholar.org/96cc/e9e93cc 46345162f 325a09086ac 22b539d40.pdf

Vittrup, B., Snider, S., Rose, K. K., Rippy, J. 2014. Parental Perceptions of the Role of Media and Technology in their Young Children's Lives. *Journal of Early Childhood Research.* 14(1), 43-54. doi: 10.1177/1476718X14523749.

Vivek, A., Saranya D. 2012. Harmful Effects of Media on Children and Adolescents. *Journal of Indian Association Child Adolescence Mental Health.* 8(2), 38-45.

Waldman, M., Nicholson, S., Adilov, N. 2006 'Does Television cause Autism?', Study Presented to National Bureau of Economic Research Health Conference, Working Paper No. 12632, October; revised December 2006. Retrieved 13th May 2017 from https://www.researchgate.net/publication/5187483_Does_Television_Cause_Autism

Wanjohi, A.M. 2010. Theories of Language Development in Children. KENPRO Publications. Retrieved 13th May 2017 from http://www.kenpro.org/papers/theories-of-language-development-in-children.htm

Warneken, F., Tomasello, M. 2006. Altruistic helping in Human Infants and Young Chimpanzees. *Journal of Science,* 311, 1301-1303. Retrieved 10th Jan 2019 from https://www.eva.mpg.de/psycho/staff/tomas/pdf/Warn_Science.pdf

Wartella, E., Rideout, V., Lauricella, A.R., Connell, S.L. 2013. Parenting in the Age of Digital Technology – A National Survey. Northwestern University. Retrieved 1st May 2018 from https://cmhd. northwestern.edu/wp-content/uploads/2015/06/Parenting Age Digital Technology.REVISED.FINAL_.2014.pdf

Wellman, B., Haase, A.Q., Witte, J., Hampton, K. 2001. "Does the Internet Increase, Decrease, or Supplement Social Capital?" *Journal of American Behavioral Scientist.* 45(3):436-455.

Wilsenach, C., Makaure P., 2018. 'Gender Effects on Phonological Processing and Reading Development in Northern Sotho Children Learning to Read in English: A Case Study of Grade 3 learners', *South African Journal of Childhood Education.* 8(1), a546. https://doi.org/10.4102/sajce.V8i1.546.

Winpenny, E.M., Marteau, T.M., Nolte, E. 2014. Exposure of Children and Adolescents to Alcohol Marketing on Social media websites. *Journal of Alcohol.* 49(2), 154-159.

Wolfe, S., Flewitt, R. 2010. New Technologies, New Multimodal Literacy Practices and Young Children's Metacognitive Development. *Cambridge Journal of Education*, 40(4), 387-399. doi: 10.1080/0305764x.2010.526589

Young Children Report. 2011. Young Children Consuming More Digital Media. Retrieved 9th June 2012 from http://www.emarketer.com/Article/Young-Children-Consuming-More-DigitalMedia/1008435

Zimmerman, F.J., Christakis, D.A. 2005. Children's Television viewing and Cognitive Outcomes – a Longitudinal analysis of National Data. *Journal of JAMA Pediatrics*. 159(7), 619-625.

Zimmerman, F.J., Christakis, D.A., Meltzoff, A.N. 2007. Associations between Media Viewing and Language Development in Children under Age 2 years. *Journal of Pediatrics*, 151, 364-368. http://dx.doi.org/10.1016/j.jpeds.2007.04.071

Index

❑ ❑ ❑ ❑ ❑